"The story had everything: A mass poisoning—during a church social hour, no less—that left one man dead and was unlike anything that had ever been seen in the United States . . . [and] a quirky, close-knit community that was a cross between Cabot Cove and Lake Wobegon . . . In the weeks following the poisoning, no one was talking. But that didn't stop Christine Young. *A Bitter Brew* is Young's . . . account of what was really going on behind closed doors at Gustaf Adolph."

—*Portland Press Herald*

"Riveting . . . . Sleuthing is in Young's blood."

—*The Forecaster*

"Young unfurls the tale in tantalizing detail worthy of the best mystery writers. [Her] descriptions of the northern Maine landscape and her cast of characters are dead-on. She is especially good at capturing the personalities of the detectives and state officials who were involved in the case."

—*Bangor Daily News*

"A compelling book about the bizarre case."

—*The Boston Globe*

"Young illuminates the congregation's strong Swedish roots, as well as its ugly infighting."

—*Publishers Weekly*

A BITTER BREW

Faith, Power, and Poison
in a Small New England Town

Christine Ellen Young

BERKLEY BOOKS, NEW YORK

THE BERKLEY PUBLISHING GROUP
Published by the Penguin Group
Penguin Group (USA) Inc.
375 Hudson Street, New York, New York 10014, USA
Penguin Group (Canada), 90 Eglinton Avenue East, Suite 700, Toronto, Ontario M4P 2Y3, Canada
(a division of Pearson Penguin Canada Inc.)
Penguin Books Ltd., 80 Strand, London WC2R 0RL, England
Penguin Group Ireland, 25 St. Stephen's Green, Dublin 2, Ireland (a division of Penguin Books Ltd.)
Penguin Group (Australia), 250 Camberwell Road, Camberwell, Victoria 3124, Australia
(a division of Pearson Australia Group Pty. Ltd.)
Penguin Books India Pvt. Ltd., 11 Community Centre, Panchsheel Park, New Delhi—110 017, India
Penguin Group (NZ), Cnr. Airborne and Rosedale Roads, Albany, Auckland 1310, New Zealand
(a division of Pearson New Zealand Ltd.)
Penguin Books (South Africa) (Pty.) Ltd., 24 Sturdee Avenue, Rosebank, Johannesburg 2196,
South Africa

Penguin Books Ltd., Registered Offices: 80 Strand, London, WC2R 0RL, England

A BITTER BREW

A Berkley Book / published by arrangement with the author

PUBLISHER'S NOTE: As of this writing, no one has been indicted or criminally charged in the case of the New Sweden arsenic poisoning. The unwillingness of investigators to accept the confessed killer's declaration that he acted alone has understandably generated fear, suspicion, gossip, and even hysteria in a small town where everybody knows everybody. This book tells that story and recounts the rumors, finger-pointing, and accusations, often made without any factual basis, that have sometimes turned neighbor against neighbor. Reporting what has been said by various townspeople is intended simply to illustrate how the crime has disrupted this formerly close-knit community, and is not an endorsement or validation of any of the unsubstantiated theories and suppositions that have been expressed.

PRINTING HISTORY
Berkley hardcover edition / April 2005
Berkley mass-market edition / March 2006

Copyright © 2005 by Christine Ellen Young
"Don't Piss Off a Lutheran" by Tom Flannery copyright © 2003 by Tom Flannery/BMI
www.songaweek.com
Cover design by George Long; Cover art by Franco Accornero; Church photo © A.P. Photo
Book design by Kristin del Rosario

ISBN: 0-425-20918-0

BERKLEY®
Berkley Books are published by The Berkley Publishing Group,
a division of Penguin Group (USA) Inc.,
375 Hudson Street, New York, New York 10014.
BERKLEY is a registered trademark of Penguin Group (USA) Inc.
The "B" design is a trademark belonging to Penguin Group (USA) Inc.

PRINTED IN THE UNITED STATES OF AMERICA

10 9 8 7 6 5 4 3 2 1

Author's Note

This is a work of nonfiction, but I have used pseudonyms for some of the characters in this book to protect their privacy. Conversations, thoughts, reflections, and scenes are drawn from interviews with the people involved. In the interest of protecting sources, the four detectives who meet to discuss the case are composite characters with pseudonyms, and their small talk and banter are imaginary; but all of the facts, theories, evidence, and interviews pertaining to the case are written as they were described to me.

For my husband

Acknowledgments

I first wish to thank my husband, John Pertel, for your unwavering love and for giving me a life beyond my wildest dreams.

To my children, Anna, Noah, Allie, and Katelynn, thank you for putting up with an absentee mom and for making me happy every single day.

To my beautiful sister, Connie Krinsky, thank you for always being on my side no matter what, and for being the very best sister in the world. I admire you more than anyone I know.

To my dad, Raymond Joseph Young, thank you for teaching me to love good books and for telling me I could be whatever I wanted.

To Marcia Pertel and the Loose Women Book Club, thank you for cheering me on.

Lynn Holst, my loving friend of twenty years, thank you for keeping me on the straight and narrow—as best you could—and for getting this book idea off the ground.

Lester Beaupre, thank you for your courage, your friendship, and for always cracking me up.

Thank you, Ralph Ostlund, for the beautiful mornings spent skiing around Madawaska Lake, for dancing me under the table, and for being brave enough to take me to church.

Dave Socoby, thank you for your remarkable insight, your wonderful sense of humor, and your flawless integrity.

Debbie Blanchette, thank you for trusting me.

Thank you, Beth Salisbury, for being a breath of fresh New York air.

Thank you, Bill Stokes, for saying as much as you could, even though you hate to say anything.

Jerry Nelson, thank you for the nice long chats at Madawaska Lake and for sharing your incredible historical knowledge.

Gale and Nancy Doody, thank you for letting me live in your nice warm house on Madawaska Lake.

Ellen Geiger, my literary agent—thank you for keeping the faith, for your encouragement, your guidance, and for everything else you have done on my behalf. You are the best—the very best.

Finally, to my editor, Natalee Rosenstein, thank you for your patience.

"Don't Piss Off a Lutheran"
by Tom Flannery

Gentle souls well I guess that's true
churchgoers wave at the sight of you
caution is a word it's not a sin
so don't piss off a Lutheran

Wallflowers at a dance watch out for these
when you pass 'em by say "excuse me please"
they harbor grudges in places you've never been
so don't piss off a Lutheran

Bring your own drinks to the social please
or you may end up on your knees
but you won't be praying to the Lord above
you'll be dying in the name of love

Religion is a strange and scary thing
when you die for the things you're believing in
be your own man and stick out your chin
but don't piss off a Lutheran

Be your own man and stick out your chin
but don't piss off a Lutheran

Introduction

On July 23, 1870, twenty-two men, eleven women, and eighteen children arrived from Sweden in the northern Maine woods, weary from a difficult monthlong journey and eager to settle into twenty-five cabins and land parcels they had been promised by William Widgery Thomas of Portland. Thomas had first traveled to Sweden as a diplomatic courier for President Abraham Lincoln, and after the Civil War, having been appointed Maine's "Commissioner of Immigration" by Governor Joshua Chamberlain, he returned to Sweden on a mission to recruit.

Those fifty-one colonists did not get what they expected; the state had managed to construct only six of the twenty-five cabins it had promised. Undaunted, they made do with what they had and immediately got to work, cutting, clearing, building, and planting, and by November, they had constructed twenty-six houses, planted sixteen acres of winter wheat and rye, and harvested two acres of turnips.

Over the next few years there were several more waves of immigration from Sweden, although life in America was far from easy. The year 1874 brought a meager harvest, forest fires, and an end to state assistance, but these rugged, determined people carried on, and 1876 saw the first round of American naturalizations. By 1895, there were 1,452 members of Maine's Swedish Colony, spread out over Woodland, Caribou, Perham, Westmanland, and New Sweden.

The First Swedish Evangelical Lutheran Church was founded in August 1871 with the Reverend Andrew Wiren serving as pastor. The yellow chapel on Capitol Hill Road was dedicated July 23, 1880. In July 1896, the name was changed to Gustaf Adolph—after King Gustav II Adolf, born in Sweden in 1594, destined to lead his country through a string of victories during the Thirty Years War. He was killed in 1632 in the Battle of Lutzen, but sixteen years later, in the Peace of Westfalia, Sweden was established as a great power for the first time in history.

When it was incorporated in 1895, New Sweden, Maine, had a population of six hundred, and in 2003 it wasn't much higher—only six hundred twenty-one.

Such is the nature of New Sweden; change comes slowly, if at all, as if life were just as it should be and as it should stay. These people have bonded for generations, their lives interwoven into a thick, tight, and sturdy fabric that does not easily tear or fray, and serves nicely as a curtain to an intrusive world.

In 2003, as a television reporter, I became a most unwelcome intruder, poking my nose into an incident that was New Sweden's equivalent of 9/11—the poisoning of sixteen worshipers who drank coffee on Sunday, April 27, at Gustaf Adolph Evangelical Lutheran Church.

It was difficult for any of us in the media to understand or appreciate the impact of the poisoning and the subsequent death of Walter Reid Morrill on this tiny community, where rolling hills, sprawling farms, and golden-pink skies are the picture of heaven itself. We breezed into northern Aroostook County with cameras, microphones, and deadlines, expecting people to talk about what had happened, the problems that had led up to it, and to express their anger and hurt. Instead, they told us that no one among them was capable of deliberately committing such an act; that notion, in fact, had never even crossed their minds. It had to be an accident, they said, until law enforcement told them otherwise.

When police announced that Reid Morrill's death was a homicide, it meant that someone among them had not only committed a murder, but had attempted a mass murder. Even today, I don't believe an outsider can begin to comprehend the devastation that news brought to this community, or how the onslaught of media attention worsened its trauma. The police told reporters about spats, feuds, politics, and hard feelings, and we wanted the details. Yet nobody was talking. We asked one another, what is wrong with these people? Why won't they talk about this? Don't they understand that someone has tried to kill them? The police had similar feelings: "These people are *weird*," said one detective who had tried in vain to penetrate this seemingly closed society.

As I struggled to understand their silence and apparent denial, I came up with an analogy. What if, I thought, there had been a murder within my own family? And what if suddenly, reporters and photographers from all over the world were camped out on my front lawn, knocking on my door, asking me questions about the feuds, hard feelings, and disagreements that had occurred within my own home? I know exactly what I would do. I would tell them to leave us alone, and I would slam the door. I would despise each and every one of them for preying on the tragedy and heartbreak that had befallen my family.

It was not only the poisoning that made this story fascinating; it was the fact that such a hideous act had been committed in a church. I have long been captivated by stories that involve religion and the hypocrisy that so often corrupts genuine faith. I also found this area of Maine, which is five hours north of my home, uncommonly rich in material: its unusual history, respect for tradition, geographic beauty, and most of all, its colorful, quirky characters. When I returned home from my television assignment, I decided to propose this book. I had never written a book, but it had long been my dream, and during a thirteen-year career as an investigative reporter, I had enjoyed much success in getting the stories that were hard to crack. I thought that once the media hordes had moved on to the next day's headlines, the people of New Sweden would begin to open up and help me write the story of what had happened to them and why.

Eventually, I did get the story, but not without many stumbles and miscalculations. At Gustaf Adolph, an aggressive reporter in a black leather jacket is regarded with about as much fondness as a drug dealer in a schoolyard. During the spring, summer, and fall of 2003, I took many trips to New Sweden and had innumerable doors slammed in my face and phones hung up in my ear. I tried repeatedly to interview church members who appeared to be key figures in the investigation, including Norma Bondeson, Carl Bondeson, and Fran Ruggles, all to no avail.

At last, bless them, Ralph Ostlund and Lester Beaupre, both survivors of the poisoning, agreed to talk to me and tell me their stories, and we became friends. In the winter of 2004, I rented a house on Madawaska Lake, and spent many mornings cross-country skiing with Ralph and drinking coffee at the local hangout, Stan's. But after three weeks in Aroostook County and ten months after the poisoning, I knew that I still did not have the story.

Finally, one night, I picked up the phone and called Herman Fisher, the man who made the coffee, who served as church council president, and who nearly died from acute arsenic poisoning. I told him to picture me on my knees, begging for an interview. He, his wife, Karla, and Erica and Lois Anderson all agreed to speak to me, on the record, over a period of three days. They told me that had I called only weeks earlier, they would have refused, because time needed to pass before they were ready to talk. They also allowed me to tape-record their interviews, for which I am ever thankful, for without these tapes, I might not have later believed what I had heard, and neither, I reckon, would you.

Christine Ellen Young
August 2004

"Peace Be with You"

Stubborn mounds of snow dotted the brownish-green lawn of Gustaf Adolph Evangelical Lutheran Church in New Sweden, Maine, even though it was April 27, 2003, the first Sunday after Easter. The morning sun was doing its best to melt winter into spring, but the air was chilly. It is said that Aroostook County has two seasons—winter and July. Herman and Karla Fisher arrived at the weatherbeaten stucco chapel at about a quarter of nine, after a brisk walk from their home just down Capitol Hill Road. Services didn't begin until 9:15, but Herman had to make the coffee. He opened the side door facing the old parsonage, and the couple went inside. Karla was the organist, so she headed into the red-carpeted sanctuary to gather the day's music. Ushers Carl and Dale Anderson had already arrived and were stacking bulletins on a table near the front door. Karla flipped a wall switch, and crystal chandeliers flickered multicolored prisms over sturdy white pews. She waved to the ushers and sat down. She had already told Herman that she was going straight home after the service. Their nineteen-year-old son, Barrett, was in the Army—military police.

He had been shipped to Iraq two months earlier, and his parents had not heard from him in three weeks. Karla was in no mood for church chat.

"I don't want to talk to anybody; I don't want anybody to ask me anything," she had told her husband before they left the house. "I'll go to church, play the organ, and I'm coming home."

For weeks, Karla had been watching television day and night—CNN, ABC, you name it—all war, all the time. Barrett was in Iraq, heaven knows where—he wasn't allowed to say. He could be in Mosul, where Kurds and Arabs had been shooting at one another since Saddam's overthrow. It was chaos. Looting was rampant; a couple dozen people had been killed and hundreds wounded by gunfire. The United States had just dispatched the military police to help restore calm. Barrett's unit could be there. Or he could be serving as a guard in one of those Iraqi prison hellholes. Karla was crazed with anxiety. Just play the hymns, she told herself, and go straight home. He might just call today.

Herman went into the kitchen to start the coffee and took the fifty-cup aluminum coffee urn off the counter. *Let's see, about thirty-five cups*, he thought, enough for social hour and the church council meeting afterward. Two years of bickering and haggling, and finally a decision would be made today on the furnace. As council president, Herman would be glad to have that issue out of his sparse white hair once and for all. He filled the pot about two-thirds with water, nice and cold—the only way to make decent coffee—then set it back on the counter. He put the metal stem back into the urn, lined the basket with a paper filter to trap the grounds, then reached to the cupboard above the sink and took out the can of Friendship Blend coffee. He scooped the grounds into the basket, put the cover back on the pot, and plugged it in. As the church bell tolled, the coffee brewed.

The Strife Is O'er, the Battle Done. If only it were so, Karla thought as she played the morning's processional hymn. The war in Iraq had just begun, and her son was at the start of a yearlong tour of duty. She couldn't wait to finish the service and get home. Alana Margeson was serving as lay minister, and the speaker today was Mary Lou Brown, a sixty-four-year-old seminary student from nearby Caribou. The gospel was John, chapter 20, verse 19: "The first day of the week . . . where the disciples were assembled . . . came Jesus and stood in the midst, and saith unto them, 'Peace be unto you.'"

Thank God the sermon was short, Karla thought, although they had been mercifully brief for a good two years, ever since the Reverend Scottie Burkhalter had packed up and moved his wife, Myra, and their five kids to Tennessee— leaving some members wanting to tell him not to let the door hit him on his born-again Southern ass. This small congregation didn't need a full-time pastor anyway. Since Burkhalter left, various members had performed the liturgy each week, and a visiting speaker or someone from the flock would deliver the sermon. If some of these homilies came from the Internet, so what? It worked just fine, and it saved GA about twenty-eight grand a year.

The service had taken exactly an hour. As Karla played the recessional hymn, twenty-seven worshipers filed into Svea Hall, a big, open space with high tin ceilings and walls lined with memories of births, anniversaries, communions, confirmations, weddings, and Sunday school, and with rows of obedient Lutheran children smiling dutifully in faded black-and-white photographs.

As always, Herman headed up the queue at the coffeepot; on another table was punch and Kool-Aid for the kids. Herman filled his disposable cup, bypassed the creamer and sweeteners, and grabbed a tuna sandwich left over from Saturday's bake sale. The council meeting started at ten-thirty in the church study, and he went in there to wait. Sipping his coffee, Herman noticed it was unusually strong, but that was no big deal. A former Navy man, he had been everywhere and had drunk all kinds of coffee, from very bad to very good. This coffee was bad. And he had made it himself. Oh, well, better luck next time. As he scanned the bids for the new furnace, Herman finished off the cup.

In Svea Hall, Alana Margeson didn't have time for coffee; she was searching for a notebook and pen to take council minutes. Erich, her husband, got himself a cup. Their two-year-old son, Noah, sometimes asked for a sip, but today he wasn't interested. He wanted Kool-Aid. *Just as well,* Erich thought, *this coffee has a strange aftertaste.* Erich had an almost tingling sensation in his mouth. Dishwashing detergent, maybe? No, it was stronger than that. Maybe someone had scrubbed the pot with a chemical compound to remove the mineral deposits. New Sweden's hard water can be tough on utensils. *But it* is *drinkable,* Erich thought, swallowing it down.

Lester Beaupre was even hungrier than usual after the service and happy to see all the bake-sale goodies. He loved that about Gustaf Adolph—sweets after the service. Every week someone would sign up to make coffee and bring refreshments—sometimes only a bag of doughnuts one of the guys had picked up at the last minute, but occasionally an elaborate tray of beautiful pastries created by Lois Anderson or Karla Fisher, or an assortment of Ralph Ostlund's blueberry, apple, and strawberry-rhubarb pies. At GA there was always something to munch on and coffee to sip during social hour, and for Lester, it made attending church fun. He had grown up in Sacred Heart Roman Catholic Parish in Caribou, where people couldn't wait to get out the door after Sunday Mass. The priest would no sooner raise his hand for the final blessing, "May the Lord be—" and *boom,* it was a stampede. Out the door they went. Church was an obligation there, not a social event like it was here. So when Lester married Louise and she wanted him to attend Gustaf Adolph, he obliged. What the heck. They were almost the same anyway, the Catholics and the Lutherans. And besides, the Lutherans made it a lot easier for a Catholic to join them than the other way around. Lester took two sandwiches, tuna and egg salad, and decided to splurge on a slice of banana bread for dessert. The banana bread was nice and sweet, with icing on top, and he was chasing it down with coffee when he spotted Reid Morrill standing next to the bookcase. Just a few months earlier, Reid had undergone quintuple bypass surgery, a risky procedure for a man of seventy-eight. Although his recovery hadn't been easy, he was ever the good-natured prankster who loved to kid around. Now Reid was grimacing theatrically and peering into his cup.

"Man, what's in this coffee?" he exclaimed. "It tastes like poison!"

Lester laughed, but once he finished the banana bread, he noticed that the coffee did taste pretty awful.

June Greenier was chatting with Shirley Erickson when she became aware of the dreadful taste in her cup. "Shirley, is it my imagination, or is there something wrong with this?"

Shirley took a sip. "My goodness," she said, "this is just terrible. Bitter!"

Lois Anderson glanced at her watch as she waited in Svea Hall to teach a Sunday school class. *I've got a good ten minutes or so*, she thought. *I think I'll get myself some coffee and a bite to eat.* She went into the kitchen, picked up a tuna sandwich, and got in line. By the time she got to the pot, the coffee was running low, and the flow from the spigot slowed to a trickle as she filled her cup. Josh Doucette, her fifteen-year-old grandnephew, was waiting behind her impatiently.

"Well, I guess I'll have Kool-Aid today," he groused, then went and poured the neon beverage from a pitcher.

Lois took a bite of her sandwich. *My goodness*, she

thought, *this tuna is the worst thing I've ever tasted. It has the consistency of cat food.* She turned to her daughter Alicia. "Look," she joked, "if you go upstairs and I'm lying there, it's the fish sandwich. Remember—it's the fish sandwich."

Lois drank half the coffee, which didn't taste much better, and threw the rest in the trash.

"Council meeting—let's go!" someone yelled.

Council member Bob Bengston grabbed coffee and headed into the study. After sitting down at the long table, he took a swallow and grimaced. "Ugh. This is the worst coffee I've ever tasted."

"I took that to heart," Herman later joked. "I felt insulted."

Dale Anderson sat down and drank from his own cup. *Tastes like the creamer is going bad*, he thought. But he finished it anyway. Dale's older brother Carl sat down beside him. Carl usually had coffee, but this morning he had become so wrapped up in conversation that he'd never made it to the kitchen. Then Dick Ruggles came in looking pale and queasy. He went to the restroom and came back just as the meeting was getting under way.

Upstairs, Lois was starting opening prayers with a handful of second graders when she had an attack of severe nausea. She excused herself, went downstairs, stepped outside, and vomited. She waited a few moments before going back upstairs to the classroom. *I'm okay now*, she thought. But no sooner had she begun the day's lesson when the nausea hit her again.

"You're going to have to excuse me, but I need to—" she told the kids, and she grabbed a bag of markers and dumped them out on a table. She ran from the room, sat on the stairs, and vomited into the bag. This time, she couldn't even move. Her daughter Kristi was teaching in the next room, so Lois called out, "Kristi, will you come get my kids working?"

Kristi took over the lesson, and Lois sat on the stairs. She could not stop throwing up. Then Josh, who was usually in charge of counting donations and taking attendance, came up the stairs. "Josh, will you teach my class?" Lois asked him. "I've got to go home, I'm so sick."

As Josh took over the class of puzzled children, Lois stumbled downstairs and into the bathroom.

It took only fifteen minutes for the church council to select Dead River Oil to supply the new furnace. Finally, there had been a consensus: Fix the furnace in the church, and buy a new furnace for the parsonage. Dead River offered the best bang for the buck, the council decided. Small voices still chanted from the Sunday school as councilors donned their coats and left the church. Herman was glad the meeting had been brief, but before he could go home, he had to wash out the coffeepot. He walked back to the kitchen and unplugged the pot, then removed the lid and saw something strange. The metal stem had come out of its fitting, and the filter basket was off the stem and tipped over. A lot of the grounds had spilled, although some had remained in the basket. He wondered what the heck had happened. Maybe that's why the coffee tasted so bad. He shrugged, rinsed out the pot, put it back on the shelf, and then put on his coat and left.

The air was still nippy as Herman walked home. As he entered through the side door into the family room, a delicious aroma greeted him. Karla was in the kitchen preparing scrambled eggs, hash browns, and bacon. *Son of a gun, gonna have me a good breakfast*, he thought. Then it hit him.

"Karla, I'm sorry, I can't eat," he said, then ran to the bathroom.

It's that friggin' tuna sandwich, Herman thought. He started to leave the bathroom, and then he started heaving again. Then again. *Geez, maybe I ought to go lie down; maybe if I sleep, it'll go away.* He went into the bedroom, took off his shoes, and lay down. But try as he might, Herman could not sleep. His insides were churning.

Lois Anderson didn't even say hello to her husband, Carl, or their daughters, Erica Grace and Alicia, when she got home from Sunday school. She lurched through the door and into the bathroom. Carl and Alicia had both attended church, but neither was ill. Erica had skipped church, opting instead to sleep late after some late-night partying at the American Legion's annual pig roast. Practically all of New Sweden had attended. Erica had been with a large group of friends, as well as various aunts, uncles, and cousins. Reid Morrill attended, as did Ralph Ostlund, who was almost eighty and danced up a storm. Everyone had a blast. Now Erica was nursing a hangover, but she didn't feel nearly as bad as her mother looked.

"I'm going upstairs to take a nap," Lois said, and she slowly climbed the stairs to her bedroom.

At about three o'clock, the telephone awakened Lois. It was Barbara Bondeson. "A bunch of people from church are getting sick," Barbara told her. "Reid went to the hospital."

"Really?" Lois said. "I feel terrible too; I've been sick all morning. I think it's food poisoning from a bad tuna sandwich. But I don't want to go to the hospital now. I'll just wait and see how I feel later on."

Lois hung up, and Erica called. She was in Stockholm, about five minutes away, visiting cousins. People had been calling there all afternoon about the rash of sickness among GA churchgoers, and Erica had become worried about her mother, who was diabetic.

"Maybe you should go to the hospital, Mom," Erica said. "It's getting near suppertime, and you haven't eaten."

"I'm waiting to see," Lois replied, but she was worried. *If I don't feel well enough to eat by suppertime*, she thought, *I don't know if I can take my insulin.*

"Don't wait too long, Mom. I mean it." Erica hung up and called her uncle Dale's house. His wife, Penny, answered the phone.

"He's been on the couch heaving ever since he got home from church," Penny said. "He refuses to go to the hospital. He says it will pass in a day or two."

"Well, I'm going to keep after my mom," Erica said. "And you keep an eye on Uncle Dale. If we have to drag them to the hospital, we will."

At five o'clock, Lois was still too sick to eat. She called Cary Medical Center and asked for the triage nurse. "I can't keep anything down," Lois told the nurse. "I don't think I should take my insulin; I'm going to be here with a sugar low because I can't keep any food down."

"You need to come in and let a doctor see you," the nurse said. "Come right away."

"I'll drive you to the hospital," Alicia said. "Let's go."

"Carl didn't think I was that sick," Lois remembered later with a laugh. "He would have let me die right there."

God and the Doctors

Julie Adler rarely missed Sunday service, but this morning she had no choice. She had to take care of Melvin, her husband of almost fifty years. In fact, their golden anniversary was coming up in only a few days, and Gustaf Adolph was having a celebration in Svea Hall. It was sure to be bittersweet. Once a hardy, robust farmer, Melvin now suffered from chronic pulmonary obstruction, was on oxygen twenty-four hours a day, and needed help getting around. For Julie to get away, even for church, required backup from family members, and today nobody had been available.

At around 5 P.M., the phone rang.

"Julie? It's Barb. Listen, a bunch of people got sick today after church—very sick." Julie Adler and Barbara Bondeson had known one another for most of their lives. Both women were active in Gustaf Adolph's Women's Evangelical Lutheran Church Association, or WELCA, which had sponsored Saturday's bake sale.

"Barb, what are you talking about?" Julie said. "I wasn't even at church today."

"I know. But Fran and Dick were there. And they're not doing so well. I just called their house."

"Fran and Dick?" Fran Ruggles was Julie's sister, and Dick was her husband. Both were in their sixties.

"Yes," Barbara said. "I called over there and Fran could barely talk."

Julie was becoming alarmed. "Well, what is it? Food poisoning? Did they eat something bad? Who else is sick?"

"Herman, Erich, Ralph, Reid, Lois," Barbara told her. "They all stayed for fellowship hour."

Julie hung up and told Melvin she'd be back as soon as she could. Then she jumped in her car and drove to her sister's house. When Julie walked through the door, she took one look at Fran and Dick and gasped.

Dick was lying on the couch, vomiting into a bucket. His face was ghostly white. So was Fran's. She was sitting in a chair, doubled over, her eyes wide and frightened. Julie, a retired nurse, worried that they were both dehydrated. "You two are going to the hospital with me right now!" she ordered. But Dick was so weak he couldn't walk, and Julie didn't know how she was going to get him into the car. She called her son Tim and asked him to come over right away. Pacing back and forth as she waited, Julie tried to figure out what had happened. She thought of the bake sale.

"What did you eat at church today? What kind of stuff was out?" She wondered about the leftover egg salad and tuna sandwiches. Maybe someone had forgotten to refrigerate them.

"We didn't eat anything," Fran said weakly. "All Dick and I had was coffee."

Coffee? I've never heard of coffee causing food poisoning, Julie thought.

It took both Julie and Tim, with considerable lifting and dragging, to get Dick into her car. The bucket came too. Fran was quiet, but her skin looked clammy, with a greenish-white tone. Julie sent Tim to stay with Melvin, and she got in the car and sped toward Caribou.

.   .   .

At five-thirty, the Fishers' daughter, Amber, arrived at the house. She was tanned and smiling, having just returned from a weeklong Caribbean cruise.

"Has Barrett called?" she asked Karla, giving her mother a kiss on the cheek.

"Not yet," Karla replied, hugging her daughter. She took a step back and gave Amber the once-over. "Look at you, all tanned and rested."

"Where's Dad?"

"Upstairs. He's been sick since he got home from church. Go on up and see how he's doing."

As Amber lugged her suitcase up the stairs, Fran Ruggles called. Her voice was weak. "Karla, we're going to the emergency room," she said. "Dick and I are both very ill, and so are a lot of other people who were at church this morning. I really encourage you to get Herman to a hospital."

Something about Fran's voice frightened Karla. She hung up and went up to the bedroom, where Amber was sitting with her father. "Herman, I'm driving you to the hospital," she said. "We have to leave right now."

Karla took deep breaths to steady her nerves as she steered the car around the familiar bends of New Sweden Road leading to Caribou. It was a ten-mile drive to Cary Medical Center. Herman had resisted going, but not for long. He had never felt this rotten in his life. At sixty-two, he had always been lucky with his health. Now, after a lousy cup of coffee and a tuna sandwich, he was deathly ill. Maybe it was food poisoning. Or, as someone suggested during the day's phone-call frenzy, maybe the sewer had backed up into the church well. Herman glanced at Karla. "I guess when they said the coffee tasted like shit, they really meant it, huh?" Karla cackled. She could never resist her husband's wicked sense of humor.

She pulled up to Cary Medical Center's emergency room and parked next to the entrance. "Wait," she told Herman, "I'll go get a wheelchair." But Herman was being stubborn. "No, I can walk," he barked, then he stumbled and fell to his knees. As Karla rushed to his side, she spotted Julie, who was just pulling in with Fran and Dick. "He's been like this all day!" she hollered to Julie. "I knew we should have gotten here sooner. I didn't know what to do!"

Cary's normally quiet emergency room was a cacophony of running feet, squeaking wheels, barking voices, and ringing phones. Besides Fran and Dick, three other church members were being tended to by a harried group of nurses trying to pump each one full of fluids to elevate his or her sinking blood pressure. They had severe diarrhea and violent chills, and heavy blankets were brought out to warm them. Wastebaskets full of vomit were ferried up and down the hall. A lab technician collected a parade of blood samples hoping to track down the cause.

A triage nurse took one look at Dick and sent him to an examining room, where he was attached to a heart monitor. Nurses attempted to introduce intravenous fluids to raise his blood pressure, but it was so low that his veins kept collapsing and inserting a needle took several tries. Herman and Fran were rushed into separate rooms. Both had rapidly sinking blood pressure and were also attached to IVs. *Thank heaven I missed church today*, Julie thought. As a nurse, she had worked at Cary for most of her career, but she had never witnessed a scene like this. She couldn't help but feel lucky. Fran, Dick, and Herman were violently ill; Reid, Ralph, and Erich were all on their way into intensive care. What on earth could this be?

Erica Grace showed up at the hospital even before Lois arrived. The first person she saw was Kristine Bondeson, a friendly, energetic woman who owned Down to Earth Gardens, a popular greenhouse on Route 161. Her husband, Carl, was a potato farmer who also raised cattle. Kristine was chatting with Janet and Shirley Erickson as she waited for medicine from the hospital pharmacy. Kristine's ten-year-old son, Finn, had been sick for several days.

Erica was panting as she rushed up to the women.

"My mother's on her way down," she said. "I tried to call the Fishers and got the machine. They've been waiting for Barrett to call, so Herman must be sick too. Is he here?"

"He's here, all right," Shirley replied.

Erica placed her hands on her wide hips and craned her head forward. "Where is he?" she demanded of no one in particular. She pushed a frizzy red lock from her forehead and then announced a decision: "I'm family. I'm going in."

Nobody got in Erica's way as she lumbered through the small hospital's corridors. *Okay*, she thought, *technically I'm not related to Herman, but he is my second dad. If anyone here thinks they're going to keep me out, they're dead wrong. I know this hospital well enough that I know where everything is. I know how to get around. If you don't let me in this or that door, I can come in the side, the back, through X-ray. It doesn't matter—I'll find my way in.*

Erica found Herman in a supply room, alert and upright on a portable bed, covered with a pile of blankets. Karla was with him, looking reasonably calm.

"Karla, what's going on?"

"Erica, I don't know. His blood pressure went way, way down. So they gave him something to raise it, and as soon as it kicked in, it went sky high."

Erica looked at Herman. "How are you doing?"

"I'm putting all my faith in God and the doctors," Herman said with a smile. *Me*, he thought, *who's never been sick in my life. What is this? I could just die here, and I have no idea why.*

"Hey, you'll pull through, don't worry," Erica reassured him. "Karla, I'll be back. I'm going to check on Erich."

Erich Margeson was sleeping when Erica entered his room. His wife, Alana, was sitting on a chair by the window.

"Hey, Alana, don't get scared on me now." Erica's manner was jolly. "Erich's my buddy, and so is that little boy of yours. Nothing bad is going to happen to my buddies. I've got to go find my mom, but I'll be back later."

Janet and Shirley Erickson were still in the packed waiting room when Erica returned. They were the church matriarchs, unmarried sisters who lived together, and they were almost never spoken of separately. It was "Janet and Shirley" or "the girls," or, as a detective would later call them, "the twins." They did a lot for the church, donating their time and money. When someone was sick, it was always Janet and Shirley who showed up with a casserole or a cake. They contributed to the furnace fund and saw to it that the parsonage stayed in good repair. Nobody dared mess with the girls.

"Is my mother here yet?" Erica asked. Family members had trickled into Cary's waiting room, and it was packed. Erica strained to look at the door just as Lois walked in, leaning on Alicia's arm.

"Were you at the church coffee?" a nurse asked Lois.

"Yes."

With that, the nurse escorted Lois into an examining room.

"I have diabetes and congestive heart failure," Lois told her. "I haven't been able to eat."

The nurse placed several round adhesive disks on Lois's chest to monitor her heart, and then established an IV. She told Lois to rest.

"My brother-in-law is at home on the sofa," Lois said, "and he's so sick he can't lift his head up."

"Have someone call and tell him to come here immediately."

"That sounds like a job for me," Erica chimed in.

Dr. Daniel Harrigan showed up an hour early for his 7:00 shift and found himself in the throes of a medical disaster. He had never seen anything quite like this during his twenty-one years at Cary. At fifty-two, he was an athletic man with a runner's body and shaggy dark hair, both of which made him seem younger than his age. He grew up in nearby Madawaska, the son of a physician, and as a young boy often accompanied his father on house calls. He graduated from Bowdoin College, a respected private institution on Maine's middle coast, and then went on to medical school in Canada. But Harrigan always knew that eventually he would come back to Aroostook County.

He began studying the patients' charts. He thought their symptoms seemed unusual for food poisoning, but he didn't have time to think about that now. His hands were going to be full just trying to stabilize them.

The crisis already had telephones and pagers going off in every corner of the state. Just after 7:30, Patty Carson, Cary's infection control practitioner, called Northern New England Poison Control and reached Janet Burgess. "We have an urgent situation here," Carson said. "Seven people with severe gastro symptoms after a church social. It looks like either an infectious outbreak or a toxin of some sort, but we're beginning to think a toxin is more likely, maybe something in the coffee."

"Get in touch with the church and make sure nothing is disturbed," Burgess said. "Tell them not to wash anything and not to throw anything away."

When the phone rang at Dale Anderson's house just before 8 P.M., his wife, Penny, was already worried. Dale had come home from the council meeting sick as a dog and was getting sicker by the hour. Now he was zonked out on the couch.

Dale had joined the church council in January. He had been a member of the church for twenty-five years and had lived in New Sweden all his life except when he was drafted and served an eighteen-month tour in Vietnam. After that he was a laborer, working in construction as a dump truck driver and then running heavy equipment for the Bangor and Aroostook Railroad, where he stayed for twenty-six years. Years later, he still missed that job; he was good at it.

In the winter of 2000, Dale hurt his back. He had been operating a front-end loader, clearing snow from a roadway. He backed up, and the loader fell into a hole under the snow. Dale got bounced around and a bolt struck him in the head. He suffered a concussion, sprained his neck and back, and two days later he was declared disabled.

Now he was unconscious, and his niece was on the phone sounding agitated.

"Penny, I'm at Cary, and Uncle Dale needs to get down here right now," Erica said. "My mom is here, and so are Herman, Reid and Ralph, Erich, and Fran and Dick. They're all sick. Tell Uncle Dale I'm calling back in ten minutes, and if he isn't on his way, I'm coming to get him in an ambulance."

Penny hung up. She looked at her husband. "Dale?" she said. He sat up for a moment then fell back over. Penny knew she had to get him to the hospital, but he was too weak to walk to the car; and at over six feet tall and more than two hundred pounds, he was impossible for her to lift. She called his brother Carl, who rushed over. Together they dragged him out of the house and got him into Penny's car. She turned on her flashers and headed toward Cary. They chatted for a while, but halfway there, Dale stopped responding, and Penny floored the gas pedal.

At the hospital, Erica came out with a wheelchair. Now Dale was snorting and mumbling incoherently.

"Aunt Penny, there's no way we're going to lift this man," Erica said. "Pull him up to the ambulance bay, and I'll get them to open the doors." Erica went inside and spotted some familiar hospital workers. "Carolyn," she yelled, "can you open the door?"

"We'll get it right open," Carolyn said, hurrying over, as Erica spotted someone else she knew.

"Rob," Erica hollered, "he's coming in the side door!"

Rob ran out to Penny's car. "I need help to get him on a stretcher!" he yelled. Erica followed him out to the car, where Dale was asked if he recognized his niece. Dale shook his head. He had no idea who Erica was. *Oh, my God,*

Erica thought, *they really don't know what this is. I can see it in their faces. I've got to be strong. I can't lose it now.*

"I've got to move the car," Penny said, as hospital workers laid Dale out on the stretcher and rushed him inside.

Dr. Harrigan sliced Dale's shirt away from his chest. "Get me a heart monitor!" he ordered, and a nurse ran into Lois's room and ripped the sticky disks from her chest. There were not enough portable monitors to go around, and Lois seemed to be stable, while Dale was in desperate straits. He was attached to the monitor and given oxygen. Harrigan watched the dials for a moment and gasped. "I think he's gonna code! I think he's gonna code!" The doctor leaned closer to Dale's face. "Dale, do you know your name? Do you know where you are? Dale?"

There was no response. "Get me the defibrillator!" Harrigan yelled, and a nurse scurried off. A few seconds later Dale's eyes were halfway open.

"I'm thirsty. I want something to drink. Give me something to drink," Dale mumbled. But Harrigan didn't dare give him even water, fearing it might induce more vomiting.

By the time Penny returned, Dale was starting to come back. They had pumped him full of intravenous fluids, and he was talking again. Penny had no idea how close she had come to losing her husband. "They never led me to believe that he was as sick as he was," she said later. "I was still thinking food poisoning, and that they were sending him to Bangor because they don't have any ICU beds up here. They didn't want to scare me, I guess."

It was true that Cary was bulging at the seams. Some patients would soon be leaving for Bangor, but until then, it was tight quarters. Lois was sharing a room with Dick when Erica walked in. "This is where they put you when you're bad off but they're not sure they're going to admit you," Lois said, smiling at her daughter.

A physician walked in the room and stood by Lois. He put his hand on her arm. "We're not going to keep you, Mrs. Anderson," he said. "We think you'll do fine at home."

Erica's freckled pink face turned an angry crimson. "Okay, fine," she fumed. "You send her home now, she can't eat; she's gonna throw up. So we'll be back here in the morning, and she'll be in a coma."

Erica leaned forward toward the doctor's face. Her nostrils flared, and her upper lip curled into a menacing grin. "You know what?" she snarled. "She's staying here."

Once Lois was admitted and settled in, Erica began circulating from room to room. She had a lot of buddies who needed her. *At least I'm strong enough to be here for them,* Erica thought, *unlike Alicia, who took one look at Uncle Dale and fainted right on the concrete. She just loves the attention. Granted, she's been to hell and back with aplastic anemia, but she eats up the sympathy—"Poor me, I've had a bone marrow transplant; poor me, I've had both hips replaced." Well, guess what, Alicia—my rare disease is no fun, either, nor is having a big scar in the back of my head all the way down to my shoulder blades. Okay, so we both got bad breaks with our health. But I say get on with it. Just get on with it.*

Erica Grace ceased all thoughts of her sister as she reached Reid Morrill's room. As she peeked inside, he was sitting up in his bed. "Put 'em up," he said with a grin, forming his thumb and index finger into the shape of a gun. It was a game the two of them had played since Erica was little. "Gotcha!"

Erica laughed. "Reid, you've got to get better. Golfing is coming up, and you have to help me with my swing."

A few years earlier Reid had been the talk of the town when he hit a hole-in-one at a twenty-five-thousand-dollar golf tournament. Some thought he should have won the grand prize, even though he achieved his feat in the second round of the tournament instead of the first, as was required. But Reid was just tickled that he'd gotten the ball in. Why, he couldn't even believe it himself! His technique was to simply step up to the ball, take out the appropriate club, and let 'er rip. If the ball went in, fine. If not, oh, well. It was this lighthearted, easygoing manner that made him so popular around New Sweden.

"Oh, I know, Erica, I know," Reid said. "I'm going to help you. Don't worry."

Dale's daughter, Angela, found Erica in Reid's room, and the two women went to visit Ralph Ostlund. Ralph didn't let much get him down, even though he was about to turn eighty and had lost Edith, his wife of fifty-three years, just two years earlier. "Ay-up, I coulda sat around the house, felt sorry for myself, said I had pains and all that," Ralph said. "I didn't. That wouldn't have done Edith any good. It wouldn't have done me any good either. It woulda hurt me. I would still be sittin' there. So, ay-up, life goes on no matter what happens."

Every winter Ralph cross-country skied about six hundred miles and even took part in marathons. He loved to dance, but when Edith was sick, he never got the chance. After her death, Ralph went to the Stockholm pig roast. "Nobody up there knew that I could dance," he beamed, "but they found out I could." He also enjoyed bowling, and even an occasional round of golf. "I can ski, but I can't play golf," he said. "But I can go golfin' with ya. I can hit a ball just as far as anybody I play with at times. Other times I probably hit 'em thirty yards, and I don't know where they go. Sometimes I get a triple bogey—more than that!" Yes, Ralph kept busy all right. But now he looked tired.

"We'll let you go so you can get some sleep," Angela told him.

"Okay," Ralph said, smiling. "I'm going to wait for my girls to come back."

"We'll be back to see you, Ralph," Erica assured him.

In the emergency room, plans were being made to send some patients to facilities that were larger and better equipped than Cary. Some patients would remain there, like Reid Morrill, who was deteriorating so quickly that he couldn't be moved. Lois was also staying at Cary, as was Erich Margeson. Dick, Ralph, and Dale would all go to Eastern Maine Medical Center in Bangor, which was a three-hour drive, and Herman would be sent to Maine Medical Center in Portland, six hours away. These patients needed specialized care immediately, and they would have to fly.

At about half past two in the morning, Karla was given the news that Herman was being flown to Portland. To Karla, it might as well have been Hong Kong. She didn't know Portland, and what did it matter? She was certain that Herman was going to die. She walked over to his bed and gave him a hug. "I love you, Herman," she said. Then Karla kissed her husband of fourteen years and, without saying good-bye, walked out.

Minutes after Karla left, Herman was bundled up, loaded into an ambulance, and taken to the Caribou Airport, just down the road from the hospital. The ambulance driver pulled out to the airstrip to wait for the Life Flight helicopter to arrive from Central Maine Medical Center in Lewiston. It was a long wait; the pilot had stopped in Houlton, just south of Caribou, to gas up for the return trip. Herman was conscious and alert when the chopper finally arrived. *Such a small helicopter*, he thought with alarm. *What are they going to do, just sling me on the outside like on* M*A*S*H?

"So then I'm on the stretcher, and I was freezing to death," he remembered later. "You go in sideways. You can't even see the pilot; he's in his own little enclosed space. And then there's this little cabin space, and they put you in feet first."

As the ambulance attendants loaded Herman in, they pushed a little too hard. "Gee," Herman howled, "you're going to push me right through the side of the plane here!"

The attendants adjusted Herman's position on the gurney, and when they finally got him inside the chopper, there was just enough room for him to stretch out. Two nurses were traveling with him. "Okay," one said. "We're going to put this headset on you, and if you need something, just raise your finger, okay?"

I'm all bundled up, Herman thought. *How the hell are*

they going to see my finger? "How exactly are we going to do that?" he asked.

One of the nurses loosened the blankets, got a little red light, and placed it on Herman's index finger. It was blinking. "If you need something, just lift your finger."

With that, Herman felt a rumble and heard a *chop-chop-chop* through the fresh morning air. The helicopter lifted and was off.

Amber Fisher was sleeping when Karla got home from the hospital. "They're sending your dad to Portland," Karla told her. "Has Barrett called?"

"No," Amber sighed, and she closed her eyes again.

Karla walked over to the living room window and gazed out into the darkness. "Please, God, just find a place for Herman in Bangor," she prayed. "Let him be with his friends. Let me be somewhere where at least I know somebody."

Before she said "amen" the phone rang. "Mrs. Fisher? Dr. Harrigan. We're taking Herman to Bangor. We think it's best for everyone to be together."

Karla looked upward. "Amen."

Ellie and Reid

Reid and Ellie Morrill were pulling into their driveway after church when Reid began feeling queasy. He went into the house and became violently ill. Ellie, his wife of fifty-six years, took him right over to Cary, not wanting to take any chances so soon after his open-heart surgery. Reid's stamina had improved after the surgery, but he still tired more easily than before. Even so, he never missed church if he could help it. Just last week he had prepared his traditional French toast Easter breakfast for the entire Gustaf Adolph congregation. The church was Reid's second home; in fact, it was right next door to the Morrills' house. He loved how the sun beamed off the handmade stained-glass windows, and how, on moonlit nights, murky clouds swirled around the tall wooden cross on the steeple. As Reid would tell his grandchildren, GA was beautiful—but spooky!

Over the past few years, Reid's breathtaking view of the mountains and sunset had gradually become obstructed by a maple tree in the front yard, so he asked his son Ron to come by in the spring and trim it. Ron had promised he would. It would have been hard to refuse the man who did just about anything he could for everybody else: delivering hot meals, shoveling snow, cutting the hedges, and making sure the furnace was full of oil. He was a gentle man with an easy laugh who took delight in his family.

Now Reid was lying in the Cary Medical Center emergency room, depending on a machine for every breath. There was a distant, abstract quality to the activity droning all around Ellie as she waited in the hallway for Ron to arrive from Bangor. It took her a moment to focus on the nurse now quietly trying to get her attention. "Mrs. Morrill, we're doing everything we can to make him comfortable and stabilize your husband," the nurse whispered. "He's just not responding the way we'd like. I'm so sorry to tell you this, but it doesn't look good."

For Ellie, there was no life without Reid. At twenty-one, the smart, sassy Eleanor Olsson had married her dashing young war hero on a hot Saturday afternoon—July 2, 1946—in Brownville, where both bride and groom were born. Brownville is one of seven towns in central Maine's Three Rivers Community, named for the Sebec, Pleasant, and Piscataquis Rivers. Fifty-seven years after Ellie and Reid's marriage, this community of about five thousand has preserved its homespun simplicity, enjoying such activities as the annual Spring Church Cleanup, the Kiwanis Variety Show, and bingo at the American Legion.

Ellie Olsson Morrill was the youngest child of Swedish immigrants Peter Adolph Olsson and Hulda Maria Jansson. Peter's first wife, Anna Nelson, had died in June 1915 while giving birth to a daughter. Peter gave the baby up for adoption and later married his wife's cousin, Hulda. More sorrow was to come. The couple's first son, Bernard, died of pneumonia before his first birthday; a second son, also named Bernard, drowned in 1937 at the age of fourteen. After that, the couple's sole happiness came from their daughters, Gertrude and Ellie, both of whom grew to adulthood and remained close until Gertrude's death from cancer in 1985. After almost twenty years, Ellie still missed her sister.

Walter Reid Morrill was born in 1925 to Charles McKay Morrill of Old Town and Doris Mae Dean of Barnard. He always went by his middle name, Reid, which, he would later explain, "comes from my great-grandmother in Scotland."

The Morrill family moved from Brownville to Detroit, Michigan, when Reid was about a year old and later returned to Brownville's neighboring town of Williamsburg, where Reid attended a one-room schoolhouse. Later, Charles and Doris Morrill moved their three sons and three daughters back to Brownville, where they bought a house on High Street.

In March 1943, during the height of World War II, Reid joined the Army. He served in Belgium, France, and England before his ship was torpedoed in the English Channel and his unit saved by the French Corvettes. He was honorably discharged in January 1946 and then returned to Brownville, where six months later he married Ellie.

Reid worked for a few years at odd jobs, and in 1950 he went to work for the Bangor and Aroostook Railroad as an electrician's apprentice. He and Ellie had three children between 1948 and 1955: Breta, Ronald, and Jeffrey. The family celebrated Christmas in traditional Swedish fashion, with a dinner of lutefisk—a dried fish prepared with lye—in white sauce, with potatoes, vegetables, anchovies, pigs' feet, and rice pudding. But after several holiday meals spent watching the children gag theatrically on lutefisk, Ellie finally gave in, replacing it with haddock. The rest of the supper stayed intact. "It wouldn't be Christmas without it," Ellie said.

In the early years the Morrills opened all their gifts on Christmas Eve, when the Swedish Santa Claus traditionally makes his deliveries. Only the stockings were saved for morning. Eventually, the family assumed the American custom of opening presents on Christmas Day, with Santa having visited while the children slept. Even so, the Morrills still opened one gift on Christmas Eve, a family tradition that would continue to delight their four grandchildren many years later.

In 1956, Reid completed his railroad apprenticeship, and he moved his family one hundred eighty-six miles north to Van Buren, in a cozy valley on the Canadian border covered with forests alive with deer, moose, fox, and partridge, and laced with rivers and streams teeming with salmon and trout. But before long their younger son Jeffrey was diagnosed with muscular dystrophy, and in 1960 the family moved twenty-two miles south to Caribou, where appropriate medical care was easier to come by. Eight years later the Morrills finally settled in New Sweden and bought a two-story house on Capitol Hill Road. In 1982, Jeffrey died there, of complications from muscular dystrophy. He was twenty-six. "Jeffrey lived as long as he did because my parents took such good care of him at home," Ron later said.

When Reid retired from the railroad in 1984, he took up woodworking. Later, when golfing became his passion, Reid was known to hit the links even before the last pile of snow had disappeared.

Both Ellie and Reid were active in the church. Ellie served as church organist and wrote for the Gustaf Adolph newsletter; Reid became head usher and took care of the church grounds. Every Sunday morning the Morrills walked arm in arm into the sanctuary for the service, then visited with their friends over coffee and snacks in Svea Hall.

Now at Reid's bedside, Ellie vowed to be optimistic. Just three months earlier, after all, her husband had been strong enough to survive heart surgery. And he had the prayers of his family and his friends. Although he was unconscious, attached to a respirator, Ellie was certain he could hear her voice. Clasping Reid's hand, she told him how much she loved him; how much their grandchildren needed their Poppa; that he was strong and capable and deserving of a long and wonderful life, and that she couldn't possibly go on without him.

At 3:30 A.M., Ellie and Ron were holding Reid's hands when his heart weakened to a flutter, then stopped. His lungs were filled with fluid, and his kidneys had failed. Ron, who had raced to the hospital from Bangor, stared at his dead father for a long moment. He remembered a story told by his dad many years before. Reid said that while he was in Europe during the war, one day he looked up at the sky, and he saw God.

Erica got word of Reid's death and volunteered to wait for his daughter, Breta, at the hospital's entrance. When she arrived, Erica walked Breta to her father's room, not letting on that only his body remained in the bed. As the two women approached, Ellie and Ron were standing at the door, and Breta ran up to hug them.

"How's Dad?"

"Breta, he tried so hard," Ellie said softly. "His health wasn't up to par. Do you know what I'm saying?"

Breta glanced over at Erica. "I think so," she said, her eyes locked on Erica's. "I'm not sure."

Erica stared back at Breta for a moment and nodded. She turned and walked away, hearing the sobs of Reid's wife and daughter, and the consoling whispers of his son.

Arsenic and Other Suspects

At 3:30 A.M., Dr. Anthony Tomassoni was getting a rare, deep sleep when his pager went off. It would be some time before Tomassoni would sleep that soundly again. Two hospitals were reporting one man dead, about a dozen others with severe gastrointestinal symptoms and critically low blood pressure. They weren't responding to treatment for food poisoning. The onset had been very sudden.

Tomassoni, the medical director of the Northern New England Poison Center in Portland, Maine, rubbed his eyes and sat up in his bed. Food poisoning is common; it can happen when mayonnaise is out on the counter too long, or when a picnic sandwich is left in the sun. But the symptoms don't show up within minutes, like they apparently did here. He called his colleague, Dr. Karen Simone. As two experts in a very specialized profession, they had known each other for years. And while they have different styles—Tomassoni is a spark plug, Simone a steady flame—they complement each other so well that they sometimes finish each other's stories.

Over the phone, the two mulled over the fact that some

patients were requiring huge amounts of fluids and pressors to elevate blood pressure. They almost said it in unison: "It sounds like heavy metals."

But wait. This was a tiny rural church in Maine, not a weapons factory. As they wracked their brains for something else, Tomassoni remembered that about a month earlier, something strange had happened near Toronto. A tractor trailer loaded with twenty-one thousand pounds of a liquid herbicide, Gramoxone, had been stolen, triggering a security alert to water utilities throughout the United States. The theft sounded alarms because of Gramoxone's primary ingredient, paraquat dichloride, a toxic compound used to control weeds and grasses. A fast-acting, nonselective defoliant, paraquat kills green plant tissue on contact, and it has been used to wipe out marijuana harvests. Seriously exposed victims suffer severe abdominal pain, nausea, vomiting, and diarrhea. Acute exposure can cause kidney damage, lung convulsions, and respiratory failure. In *Toxicology, the Basic Science of Poisons*, author Curtis Klassen writes that paraquat produces "startling toxicity in humans" with a high mortality rate. For these reasons, he writes, "It is a favored suicide agent in many parts of the world."

Even more disturbing, the advisory said that while the tractor trailer had been recovered, its load of chemicals had not, and that the trailer contained valuable electronic equipment, which the thieves had left behind. Canadian authorities had immediately alerted U.S. Customs to prevent the paraquat from crossing the border. Perhaps they had been too late. New Sweden was less than forty miles from the Canadian border.

And paraquat was not the only possibility. There were other substances that could send tremors through the Office of Homeland Security: ricin, thallium, cadmium, and antimony.

Ricin, a poison derived from castor beans, has long been feared as a likely biological weapon. More deadly than cobra venom, it has no known antidote. Just a tiny amount can kill.

An intriguing Cold War mystery involves the use of ricin. Bulgarian dissident and journalist Georgi Markov was assassinated at the age of forty-nine after being speared by an umbrella tip containing a microscopic dose. Markov was an acclaimed novelist and playwright who defected in 1969 and settled in England, where he became a broadcast journalist for Radio Free Europe, the British Broadcasting Company, and the German International Broadcast Service. Richard Cummings, a former director of security for Radio Free Europe, has written extensively about Markov, whose books and plays were bitingly critical of the Communist Party and its leader, Todor Zhivkov.

According to Cummings, three attempts were made to assassinate Markov. The first was in Munich, when someone slipped poison into his cocktail at a dinner party. The second occurred on the Italian island of Sardinia when Markov and his family were on vacation. The third attempt killed Markov, and it took place in London on September 7, 1978—President Zhivkov's sixty-seventh birthday. Cummings writes that Markov was on his way to work at the BBC and was climbing the stairs to his bus stop when he felt a sudden, stinging pain in the back of his right thigh. He turned and saw a heavyset man of about forty bending to pick up a dropped umbrella. The man apologized, hailed a taxi, and left. Markov continued to his workplace and told his colleagues what had happened. He also showed them a red pimplelike wound on his thigh. By evening he had developed a high fever and was taken to a London hospital and treated for blood poisoning, but his condition worsened. He went into shock and died on September 11, 1978.

A London coroner's court ruled that Markov had been murdered by a tiny wax pellet implanted in his leg containing four hundred fifty micrograms of ricin, which was only detected because the wax did not completely melt as expected. His killer has never been found.

Thallium, a heavy metal, was another suspect on the toxicologists' list. Once used in the United States to kill insects and rodents, thallium is a bluish-white metal found in trace amounts in the earth's crust and is a by-product of smelting lead and zinc ores. Ingesting thallium at high levels may result in death, and its use was banned in the United States in 1975. But thallium is odorless and tasteless. For that reason, Tomassoni and Simone let it sink to the bottom of their list, since patients admitted to Cary Medical Center had almost all said that the coffee at church had tasted strange and bitter.

Cadmium and antimony were also dubious possibilities. A rare element, cadmium is a silver-white metal, which usually occurs sparsely in a few minerals. Most cadmium is recovered from dust collected from the gases of lead blast furnaces and from fumes eliminated during the sintering of zinc concentrates. Poisoning may result from the ingestion of an acidic food or drink prepared in a cadmium-lined cup or dish, since cadmium is often used in paint pigments, plastics, and textiles. Similarly, antimony poisoning has resulted from ingesting the glaze off a cheap enamel container after it has been partially dissolved by an acidic food, such as citrus fruit.

Narrowing the list was critical. The popular misconception about poison is that everything has an antidote. Simone and Tomassoni knew that wasn't the case. They realized that some antidotes are effective for one thing, but not another. They were also well aware that the wrong antidote can be deadly. Tomassoni and Simone were at the beginning of an intricate mystery. As investigators, they would have to work their way backward and follow the links.

Within hours, the Maine Bureau of Health announced a series of recommendations: No one should enter the church. No one should use the church water until the well could be tested. No one should eat any leftover food from the bake sale or social.

"This is the first time I've ever asked for a lock to be put on a church door," Dr. Kathleen Gensheimer, the state epidemiologist, would later say. "There was just something about the whole thing that didn't sound right." The Maine Bureau of Health was in the throes of a major forensic investigation. Because the source of the outbreak was still unknown, the state medical examiner was also brought in on the case. As the doctors waited for lab results, Patty Carson, the hospital's infection control specialist, continued to take patient histories. She was trying to zero in on the common denominator. Many had eaten sweets and sandwiches at the church bake sale the day before: tuna and egg salad, sponge cake and banana bread with icing. What struck Carson was the one thing everyone had in common: coffee.

Coffee is a staple of Swedish culture, and even very young children drink it at social gatherings. At Gustaf Adolph, the big kitchen percolator was akin to the workplace watercooler, where gossip was shared between sips. If the church coffee was contaminated, it was probably not by bacteria, which would have been killed at the boiling point. A heavy metal, such as arsenic, was more likely.

At the poison center, Tomassoni and Simone turned their attention to antidotes. The timing could not have been better. A stockpile of antidotes had arrived at Maine Medical Center in Portland just weeks earlier. The shipment was a response to September 11, after which it had become clear that Maine was not prepared for a chemical or biological attack. Tomassoni and Simone had gone to the Bureau of Health and made a twenty-minute case to Director Dora Mills that a ready supply of antidotes was critical to protect the public. Mills, a pediatrician and mother of two, was an easy sell. She obtained two hundred fifty thousand dollars from Maine's share of homeland security funds and purchased a set of antidotes for every hospital in the state.

Tomassoni never expected to see a case of arsenic poisoning in his career and never wanted to. He knew it had ghastly effects. The lungs fill up with fluid because their cells start leaking. The heart's electrical system is affected, and it can't pump well. The kidneys fail. Patients who aren't treated promptly after exposure will have neurological problems that last a lifetime. Arsenic was a brutal, terrible way to hurt someone. But even if that was the cause, nobody was saying it was deliberate. In New Sweden, that notion was absurd.

The church well would be tested for arsenic, but the water was an unlikely culprit. Arsenic is distributed throughout the earth's crust and is found in water that has flowed between arsenic-rich rocks. Drinking such water over time causes cancer of the skin, lungs, bladder, and kidney. Acute arsenic poisoning is different. It rapidly blocks the ability of cells to produce energy for vital organs such as the heart, kidneys, and lungs. Without this fuel, these organs stop functioning, and death can occur quickly.

Arsenic is not easy to detect. From the Roman Empire through the Middle Ages and the Renaissance, it was the preferred poison for eliminating enemies, rivals, lovers, and spouses. During the early Renaissance, an Italian woman named Toffana peddled a special blend of arsenic-based cosmetics, used to whiten complexions, dust wigs, and help young matrons become wealthy widows.

Some historians are convinced that Napoleon Bonaparte's British captors used arsenic to slowly poison the French hero. In *A Question of Evidence*, Colin Evans writes that Napoleon's health went into dramatic decline after he arrived on the prison island of St. Helena in 1817. Napoleon, who was fifty-one, began complaining of pain on the right side of his abdomen, swelling of his ankles, and weakness in his legs. He was diagnosed with hepatitis. Evans writes that Bonaparte's deterioration "accelerated at an alarming rate," and he was confined to his bed by 1821. He then began vomiting blood, lapsed into a coma, and died. An autopsy revealed an enlarged liver and a cancerous growth in his stomach. In his will, Bonaparte expressed his belief that someone was trying to kill him. More than a century later, a Swedish dentist set out to crack the case. In the 1950s Sten Forshufvud obtained some of Napoleon's hair and tested the strands for arsenic. The results indicated that Napoleon had ingested the toxin repeatedly, over a long period of time, as if someone might have been gradually poisoning him. The findings caused a commotion in France when they were published in 1961, and the debate over Napoleon's death continues to this day.

Arsenic remained a murder weapon throughout the twentieth century. Between 1931 and 1938 it was used in a series of deaths that came to be known as the Philadelphia Poison Ring. It was an insurance scam that involved three gangsters—brothers Herman and Paul Petrillo and Morris Bolber, who was also known as "Louie the Rabbi." The crimes took place in a South Philadelphia neighborhood with a large population of immigrants who had little or no education. Most of the twenty victims were men. Their spouses were planning to collect on life insurance policies arranged by the gangsters. The Patrillo brothers were executed for the murders, and Bolber died while serving a life sentence.

There are also stories of accidental arsenic poisoning. In 1858, twenty people in Bradford, England, died after eating a batch of peppermint lozenges. At the time, sugar was very expensive, so it was customary for confectioners to mix the sugar with an inert and cheaper substance known as daft. Unfortunately, when a druggist's assistant went into a stockroom and measured twelve pounds of white powder for the candy maker, he may have thought he was supplying daft, but he was actually providing arsenic trioxide, which is white and powdery too. The first fatalities were two children who were initially thought to have died of cholera. Then it was learned that other victims had also bought the same sweets, and investigators traced the source to the druggist's assistant. Prompt action by police is believed to have prevented other poisonings.

Early details of the New Sweden church poisoning were reported to the Northern New England Poison Control's Toxic Exposure Surveillance System and uploaded to a national poison control database in Washington, D.C. That report triggered an alert of the Centers for Disease Control and the Office of Homeland Security. Governor John Baldacci asked to participate in conference calls and to be kept apprised of important developments.

At 9 A.M. Monday, Bureau of Health sanitarian Donald McAllister was in the church kitchen collecting samples of everything, from food to trash, to be shipped out for laboratory tests. McAllister had been there only about ten minutes when two Maine State Police detectives arrived and affixed yellow tape around the building. The church had become a crime scene.

Racing the Clock

On Monday morning, Lester Beaupre had been suffering the same miserable symptoms as his fellow churchgoers ever since he'd had banana bread with coffee the day before. On Sunday evening he and his wife, Louise, had received four separate phone calls from church members who were at the hospital, and each urged Lester to go to the emergency room. Lester stubbonly refused to go, thinking the bake-sale leftovers had probably caused a rash of food poisoning.

Now Shirley Erickson was on the phone with stunning news: Reid Morrill was dead.

"Okay, Lester, this is it," Louise told him. "Put your clothes on."

The sun was bright as Louise crested the curvy hills toward Caribou, the sky Caribbean blue. As Lester gazed out the window, he saw something remarkable—fluffy white clouds with purple and pink edges. Mesmerized, he stared for two miles at the colorful puffs of cotton candy floating above. As they turned onto Route 1, Lester noticed that the snowbanks had the same vivid hues, and he became alarmed. As a cabinetmaker and carpenter, Lester had done a lot of work for a local ophthalmologist over the years. He had gleaned enough to know that when you see purple snow, you have problems.

The minute he arrived at Cary, Lester was hooked up to an IV, and a nurse checked his blood pressure. "My lip is numb—why is that?" Lester asked, his jaws chattering. He started to shiver. Doctors and nurses lifted Lester from his wheelchair, placed him on a bed, and piled heated blankets on top of him. They checked his blood pressure again.

"We've got to take him to Bangor," Lester heard someone say. Round white lights glared at him from the ceiling. *This must be an operating room*, he thought. Then he heard another voice, "Who's going to fly down with him?"

"I will," a nurse volunteered.

Lester looked at her. "Am I gonna live, or what?"

"You'll be okay once you get to Bangor," she told him. Lester doubted it. Numbness was dulling his flesh like a massive dose of Novocain, and he was certain the end was near. *This is it*, he thought. *I've been on borrowed time ever since Vietnam.* He remembered a sunny, hot morning in 1969, while he was serving in the United States Army's 196th Light Brigade, and his tank unit was traveling a short distance. The gun squad was on the first tank; Lester's squad was on the second. The gunners had just gotten a new man who happened to know one of the guys on Lester's squad from back home. The young soldier asked to switch tanks with Lester so he could sit with his old friend, and Lester agreed. No sooner had they traded places when an explosion hit the second tank. It flew up in the air, came crashing down, and landed on its side, killing every soldier on board. *If that kid hadn't asked to ride with his friend*, Lester thought, *I would be dead now too.*

An intense wave of pain jolted Lester out of the battlefield and back into his hospital bed. Ah, it felt glorious. *That's great! I'll live*, Lester thought, just as a tube slid down his throat and into his stomach. It was the last thing he would remember for three weeks.

Erica arrived home from the hospital at about 6 A.M. Monday. She was exhausted, but too jittery to sleep. Alicia had gone to meet Janet and Shirley at the church to put up signs warning people not to drink the water. They also had to unlock the door for the health bureau sanitarian. Alicia would be home any minute; then she and Erica would go back to Cary to visit their mother. Erica decided to shower; she was expecting another long, tense day of waiting for answers from doctors, public health workers, and police. Dale, Ralph, Dick, and Herman were down in Bangor. Lois had remained at Cary, along with a handful of other churchgoers who had fallen ill. Alicia came home just as Erica finished her shower. "The police talked to me," Alicia said. "They interviewed me, and they interviewed Janet and Shirley."

"What did they ask you?"

"They wanted to know if I was in church Sunday, was anyone mad at me, did I notice anything unusual, and could I think of anyone who would have done this. And they asked me if I did it."

"They asked you that?" Erica's eyes lit up like flash-bulbs. "Oh, my God! I wonder when they'll interview me." The prospect was exciting.

On Monday morning, Barrett Fisher finally called Karla from Iraq. She was on her way out the door, headed for Bangor to be with Herman. "Your dad is at Eastern Maine Medical Center," she told her son. "We don't know what's wrong. There are a dozen other people in the hospital, and nobody knows what's wrong with them, either."

Barrett promised his mother he would call again as soon as he could.

Late Monday afternoon, Tomassoni and Simone issued the order to ship the stockpiled antidotes immediately from Portland to Bangor. State police troopers were dispatched to Maine Medical Center, where they picked up more than one hundred vials of British anti-lewisite, which was employed during World War II as an anti-arsenic agent; and

Maine's entire supply of succimer, a remedy for lead poisoning and a heavy-metal antidote.

Like blue lightning, Crown Victoria cruisers streaked up the Maine Turnpike with the lifesaving cargo. Precious time was passing. Dale, Lester, and Ralph were in very critical condition, with sinking blood pressure that wasn't responding to conventional treatment. Doctors were working with the poison center to buy time. The other patients weren't doing much better, and a precise diagnosis required sophisticated equipment. That meant samples from the patients had to be tested right away. Half of the samples went to the state laboratory in Augusta, and the other half to Pennsylvania for independent analysis.

At Cary Medical Center, there had been rumblings about arsenic, but most people scoffed at the notion, including Erica. *Somebody didn't wash out the percolator well enough,* she thought, *or maybe it was something in the water.*

On Monday night, Lois called her from the hospital. She was whispering: "Erica, I'm worried. They told us it was arsenic; and I think that they think somebody did it on purpose."

Erica hadn't slept much. She had to collect her thoughts. *It has to be a farmer if it was intentional,* she reasoned. *It must be somebody who has access to arsenic.* She knew that in the past, arsenic compounds had been routinely sprayed on potato fields about three weeks before the harvest in order to kill the vines growing above ground. The practice, known as "top killing," stopped the potatoes' growth and enabled them to develop a nice, thick skin, giving them a longer storage life. In the 1960s, when the dangers of arsenic became known, it was banned for use as a top killer, and farmers began to use less toxic herbicides, or they waited for the first frost—the "killing frost."

Erica knew that although no one used arsenic anymore, the stuff could still be sitting around in somebody's cluttered barn. She also knew how deadly arsenic was. She knew because her uncle was a farmer, and she remembered how one time the top-kill sprayer had dripped, and a cow had eaten the grass where it had leaked, and the poor cow had dropped dead. Yes, sir, she was well aware of how deadly arsenic was. Around New Sweden, most everyone else knew it, too.

Dora's Dilemma

Church coffee laced with arsenic—oh, boy. Maine Bureau
of Health Director Dr. Dora Mills tried to make sense of it
as she gazed at Maranacook Lake from the front porch en-
circling her sprawling, comfortable old house. The poison
was most likely in the brewed coffee and not the canned
grounds, but investigators were not yet certain. All they had
were some leftover spills from Sunday's brew, the drinking
water, and the percolator. Although the arsenic could have
been added at the processing plant, it seemed unlikely because the canned coffee looked and smelled normal. Also,
no occurrences had been reported anywhere else. The
Northern New England Poison Center had sent the news
out over its hotline, the Food and Drug Administration
knew about it, as did the Centers for Disease Control. It
didn't seem likely that New Sweden would be the only
place to have an outbreak if the poisoning happened at the
manufacturing plant.

At 8 P.M. Monday, Dr. Mills got the verdict: The brewed
coffee was chock full of arsenic; the levels were off the
charts. She quickly made a series of calls, to Tomassoni,

the hospitals, the governor, and the Department of Public Safety.

Mills had a dilemma. As the state's health director, she felt duty bound to notify the public. But no one knew whether this incident was an accident or something more sinister. What exactly should she say? She didn't want to alarm people, but she didn't want to keep them in the dark, either—and if this did become a criminal case, she certainly didn't want to jeopardize the investigation. She had to call Bill Stokes.

If William R. Stokes were a movie character, either George Clooney or Richard Gere might suit the part. Maine's deputy attorney general is a salt-and-pepper-haired, trim, and sometimes prickly fifty-three-year-old native of Cambridge, Massachusetts, known for his sardonic wit and prosecutorial prowess. His specialty is homicide. After twenty-seven years with the Attorney General's office, Stokes has no plans to retire, since his wife surprised him with a baby boy at age forty-five. Liam is clearly the apple of his daddy's eye, and Stokes has been known to head straight from an exhausting murder trial to a testy school board meeting to vote on an issue that could affect his two kids. His concern for the welfare of children, however, is not limited to his own brood. Not long before the church poisoning, Stokes had been immersed in another high-profile case, the trial of Sally Schofield, Maine's "duct-tape killer."

Sally Schofield was a state child-protective worker with two sons when she and her husband decided to adopt a little girl. They got two instead. In September 2000, Logan and Bailey Marr, four and two years old, moved into the Schofields' home in Chelsea, Maine, with their adoptions planned for later on. But those plans went awry around suppertime on January 31, 2001, when Schofield called 911.

"My five-year-old hit her head," Schofield reported. "She's not breathing."

Logan Marr was dead on arrival at Maine General Medical Center. But it was not because she had hit her head.

When police searched the Schofields' house, they found the basement divided in half by a blanket hung in a doorway. One side was a finished family room. The other side was unfinished, with floors and walls of bare concrete. A blood-smeared high chair was tipped over on its side. Strewn across the floor were long strips of duct tape—forty-two feet in all. Stuck to the tape were clumps of long, dark hair and traces of bloody froth.

Forensic tests revealed that Logan had been tightly bound to the high chair with layers and layers of duct tape. She could not move her arms, which had been bound at her sides, straitjacket style. Her wrists had been bound together. The tape had been wrapped around her head multiple times in two directions, covering her mouth and immobilizing her jaw. The medical examiner determined she had suffocated.

Stokes was outraged. His office charged Schofield with depraved indifference, murder, and manslaughter, and he tried the case himself. Schofield was convicted of manslaughter and sentenced to twenty-eight years in the Maine Correctional Center, with eight years suspended. Stokes was disappointed; in his eyes, she was guilty of murder. "Wrapping Logan's jaw shut—that to me was the kicker," Stokes later remarked. "For what? To shut her up. To shut her up."

Bill Stokes is happy to speak his mind after a trial is over, but reporters don't have much luck before that. They generally like him because he is accessible, always courteous, and very funny. But to the exasperation of some, he will not discuss a case before trial. No exceptions. So, after a homicide, which occurs in Maine only about twenty times a year, Stokes wants investigators to shut their yaps. "I'm a big believer in the public's interest," he says. "I just don't believe in talking too much before the trial. That's when we do our talking, at a public trial."

Mills went into her living room and turned on the television. Jay Leno was on, but she wasn't paying attention. She picked up the phone book, looked up Stokes's number, and dialed. She had to alert him that Reid Morrill's death could be a homicide. She also had to figure out what to tell the public.

Stokes's opinion was predictable: nothing.

"Dora, look," he said. "The more people are talking, the better chance we have of something being said that we don't want to be public yet. That's my concern. We told the hospitals and the doctors. We make sure the public is protected, and that's that. We don't have to say anything."

Later, Stokes explained, "The dilemma we were in Monday night was we didn't really know much. We didn't know if it was an outsider; we didn't know if it was an insider, whether it was accidental. We knew very little, other than that it was arsenic, and the levels were so high that it was not normal. I was really trying to balance public health and public safety—how much are we going to publicly release? And my point was we don't say too much."

Mills understood his position. As a prosecutor, he had to be careful not to taint an investigation. If she were in his shoes, she would feel the same way. But she also felt that as a public health official, she had an ethical obligation to keep the citizens informed. "We need to say something to the public tomorrow," she argued. "How do we know that this isn't part of a broader terrorist event? Even if it was just poured into the brewed coffee, someone might be doing it somewhere else. We need to say something."

They discussed it for an hour and a half with no resolution, and decided to take it up again in the morning. Jay Leno was long over. Dora yawned, turned off the TV, and went to sleep.

Tuesday morning a news conference took place at the state capitol in Augusta. With Governor Baldacci acting as mediator, Dr. Mills and the Department of Public Safety had worked out a compromise about what to tell the public— that arsenic had caused the outbreak, and that it was a public health investigation, aided by the state police. Mills emphasized that there was no danger of additional exposure, but stopped short of saying the coffee had probably been spiked. Only a couple of reporters were there, one of them from the Associated Press. Maine State Police Lt. Dennis Appleton told the AP that the incident was "suspicious," but added there was no evidence it was criminal. Within hours, the story hit the wire.

Mills knew that some of the patients treated at Cary had already been released. She wanted them readmitted for treatment with antidotes. Shirley Erickson, who had only taken one sip of coffee, was among them. Even though she and some of the others were feeling all right, they had, after all, been poisoned.

Needles and Pills

Shortly after Herman arrived in Bangor, his kidneys shut down. Doctors had to act quickly. They decided to try dialysis, the process that cleans the blood when the kidneys cannot. It was an unorthodox treatment for arsenic poisoning, and no one was certain it would work; but at that point, the options were limited.

Herman was lucky. The dialysis dramatically lowered the arsenic levels in his blood. When his kidneys did not bounce back, doctors repeated the procedure, and the organs finally kicked in. Herman had dialysis several times, and with each treatment the arsenic levels got lower. He was not, however, out of danger. Arsenic settles in the muscles and vital organs; as such, prompt treatment with antidotes was essential. British anti-lewisite, or BAL, is a chelating agent suspended in peanut oil which is injected deep into a patient's muscles every few hours and binds with the poison, allowing it to be flushed from the body.

Herman groans at the memory. "The first two they gave it to me in my buttocks," he said. "They gave me one in each cheek; I think they did that twice. Then this male nurse comes in and says, 'I'm going to give them to you in the thigh.' Stuck me right on top of the thigh. And I said to Karla, 'They're not doing that to me again—nooo.' It's really thick. It burns."

The injections had other unpleasant effects. "They usually gave him his shot an hour before his dialysis," Karla remembers. "I came in one day, and Herman said, 'What the hell was that smell in here?' I looked at him and I said, 'Those shots. That's what stinks.'"

Lois, who was at Cary, was given two painful injections and then had an allergic reaction and turned purple—she was allergic to the antidote. So they took photos. "It was pretty embarrassing—I was naked," she said. "There was no place for modesty anywhere there. They brought the pictures back to me so I could see my face wasn't showing."

"That picture could end up in *Playboy* with anybody's head," Herman later teased her.

Lois's bad reaction to the antidote prompted her physicians to immediately contact Eastern Maine Medical Center and request a supply of an investigative drug called dimercaptopropane sulfonate. Like BAL, the drug is a chelating agent and is supposed to bind with the arsenic so it can be expelled through urination, but it had not yet been approved by the Food and Drug Administration for use as an antidote. After consulting with Dr. Anthony Tomassoni, physicians at EMMC ordered the new drug flown in from California.

As state police rushed the experimental drug up from Bangor, Lois signed the releases to get the treatment. They were expected to arrive at Cary at 6 P.M., but by half past five, Lois's allergic symptoms were gone, so she did not receive the experimental drug after all, although other church members did.

After the injected antidotes, the patients had to take pills—and lots of them, since the massive amounts of arsenic they had ingested required huge doses of antidote.

Herman had to take ten pills at a whack three times a day. The first time he took the cover off the bottle, Karla had to hold her breath because they smelled so bad. When he tried to take them he almost choked, and it took him nearly a half hour to get them all down. "When you bring these next time," he told the nurses, "bring me two glasses of milk to slick up my throat." The milk did the trick; after that, he was able to swallow the pills in ten minutes.

Each week Herman's urine was tested for arsenic, and gradually the level went down. That was the good news. The bad news was that the tests only measured the amounts expelled, and not what remained in the muscles and organs.

Lois had a different problem: Her arsenic level decreased somewhat, but then stayed constant. She knew her brother-in-law, Dale Anderson, had experienced the same thing. Someone figured out that the poison had seeped into his dentures, and Dale got rid of them. Lois did the same thing. After she was released from Cary, she saw her dentist and had her dentures replaced. After that her arsenic level went down, but it took all summer.

Lois had other health issues, too. Even before the poisoning, she suffered from congestive heart failure, diabetes, and neuropathy, which caused numbness, meaning she could have a heart attack and not even know it. At the beginning, Lois was given daily electrocardiograms; later on, she had them twice a week. She also suffered from headaches and developed a blood clot in her leg. "It just took a long time to feel better." She sighed.

Once Herman was stabilized, Karla was anxious to get in touch with their son and give him an update. Of course, she had no idea how to reach him in Iraq. She asked the Red Cross to please find Barrett and tell him his dad was okay. She also asked that he be given the number at the hospital. "I don't care what time of the day or night it is," Karla told the nurses. "If Barrett calls, you give the phone to his father."

"Well, it wasn't till after we came home," Karla later complained, "that I found out the Red Cross didn't give him the message."

There is a plausible explanation for this apparent oversight. At the time, the International Committee of the Red Cross had suspended operations in Baghdad because one of its staffers had just been caught in an ambush and shot to death. There was fighting in the streets, and medical facilities were overloaded with casualties—about a hundred an hour at one hospital alone. The organization was inundated with urgent requests for bed sheets, surgical supplies, first-aid kits, and other essentials. Baghdad had no electricity, putting water treatment plants and pumping stations out of service, and the Red Cross had been supplying twenty thousand bags of clean water a day. So it is not surprising that Barrett never received Karla's message.

A Visitor Comes to Call

When Norma Bondeson dropped in to see the poisoned
church members at Eastern Maine Medical Center, she was
about as welcome as a rattlesnake.

Norma was not the most popular woman at Gustaf
Adolph, where she was regarded by some as "from away,"
despite the fact that her great-grandparents were among
Maine's original Swedish settlers. She had been raised on a
farm in Woodland, a town bordering New Sweden to the
south, and she grew up attending Gustaf Adolph Lutheran
Church with her parents and five siblings. She left the area
after graduating from Caribou High School in 1959, became a registered nurse, and joined the Air Force. After
several moves around the country, she settled in Amesbury,
Massachusetts, about twenty miles south of New Hampshire. She retired in 2001 and began making frequent trips
back to Maine, gradually taking an increasingly active role
in the church, first becoming superintendent of the Sunday
school and then a member of the church council.

Despite her status as a council newcomer, Norma was

feisty and opinionated and didn't mince words when speaking her mind. Karla found her downright offensive: "Just nasty is what she is—just nasty."

If Karla disliked Norma Bondeson, Fran Ruggles detested her. The two were like oil and water—or better still—oil and fire. Fran and Norma had met while attending public school in Caribou, and it was loathing at first sight. "Fifty years ago Fran and Norma were beating heads," Lester Beaupre said several months after the poisoning. "That's how long they've been beating heads, those two. They have never gotten along. Never."

A half century later, nothing had changed, and the two would clash over just about anything—from Sunday school to the Christmas program—so don't even put them in the same room. Or, as Erica had once wryly suggested, "Maybe we should put them in the same room—alone."

Karla knew it wasn't always Norma's fault—not that she was defending Norma, God, no. But Fran could be a pain in the ass. "Fran said Norma always made her feel infeeerior," Karla said, rolling her eyes. "Oh, please—grow up and get the hell over it." She hooted with laughter. "Cry me a river, build me a bridge, and get over it!"

Fran was not a person to avoid conflict; and according to Karla, she seemed to relish it. "I haven't seen Fran go to any meeting where she wasn't ready to go right after somebody and fight," Karla said, recalling the time Fran and Norma had bared their fangs at each other during a Christian Education meeting. "Fran told Norma to be civil," Karla recalled. "Norma said, 'If you don't want to listen, *Frances*, that's okay.' Of course, Norma knows everybody calls Fran 'Fran.' She was trying to piss off Fran, and Fran was trying to piss off Norma." Another time the two had gotten into a heated row over setting up communion, according to Julie Adler, Fran's sister. Fran volunteered to do it for a month, and "Norma was very rude," Julie said. Since then, the two had been avoiding each other as if breathing the same air might set off a nuclear explosion.

Yes, the two of them were a spectacle, all right. If both were going to be at a church meeting, Herman would attend, just to play referee.

"You're pretty damn brave," Erica would tell him. "You're good."

On Saturday, the day before the poisoning, Norma had attended the church bake sale in the morning and had returned to Massachusetts in the afternoon. She received word of the sicknesses on Sunday night during a phone call from her brother Carl; on Monday, she heard about Reid.

Now Norma was seating herself beside Karla on the hospital's waiting room sofa. She smoothed her khaki skirt, then folded her hands in her lap. "I'm so sorry, Karla. This is terrible," she said. "How is Herman doing?"

Oh, brother, aren't we Miss Nicey-nice? Karla thought. What happened to the real Norma—the pushy, brassy, domineering bitch who wants to take over the church? Suddenly so caring and concerned, when usually she avoids me like the plague because I can't stand her and she can't stand me.

She glared at Norma: "He is not doing very well."

"You know," Norma leaned close to Karla and whispered, "I don't rule out terrorists."

Karla stared at her in disgust. "Well, I do."

Norma ignored Karla's bad manners and stood up. "I'm going to go see Herman," she said.

"Oh, no, you're not." Karla jumped up from the couch and stepped in front of Norma, who stood still for a moment, then turned and walked away. *How dare she*, Karla thought, fuming.

When Norma finished her hospital visit, she waved good-bye and headed north to the Woodland farm. It was raining when she arrived at about eight o'clock. Minutes later, two Maine State Police detectives pulled up and parked in the driveway next to an old white sedan with Massachusetts plates. As they walked across the yard, a short, gray-haired woman came outside.

"Good evening, are you Norma Bondeson?" a detective asked.

"Yes."

"I'm Detective Frank Bechard from the Maine State Police, and this is my partner, Lloyd Deschaine. We'd like to talk to you."

Norma folded her arms. "About what?"

"About what happened at the church on Sunday."

"I just got back from Massachusetts," Norma said. "I haven't eaten, and I don't even have a fire going. Now is not a good time."

"Okay," Bechard said, "we'll be back in an hour."

The detectives climbed into their cruiser, backed out of the driveway, and left.

Curtains Up

On Thursday, May 1, Reid Morrill's death was ruled a homicide. The news was delivered on CNN in a live phone interview with Steve McCausland, the wisecracking, mercurial spokesman for the Department of Public Safety. It is McCausland's job to deal with the media, to answer questions, and to be available for interviews when the brass is too busy. A diminutive, bespectacled former radio announcer, McCausland has a remarkable gift for delivering flawless sound bites in a crisp, authoritative voice. On the rare occasion when he stumbles, he will stop, clear his throat, and start over again. Once finished, he looks at the reporter, pleased with himself. "Okay?" he says, unclipping the mike from his tie. "Ten-four."

Since the poisoning, local journalists had been checking with McCausland all week in hopes of breaking any major developments, and he stole their thunder when he broke the story himself. "This was no accident," he told CNN. "We are treating this death as a homicide."

In New Sweden, the news confirmed what many already suspected. "When Reid passed away, something in my heart told me it wasn't just an act of God," Erica said. "I really thought it was intentional; I really did. I thought somebody did this on purpose, but why to Reid? Why to these people?"

Early Friday morning, Gustaf Adolph Lutheran Church served as the backdrop for live reports on CNN, ABC, and CBS. Satellite trucks were humming in the small parking lot, and big tires had sunk into the church's soft spring lawn, leaving a muddy trench. Reporters held steaming cups as they shivered between live shots.

Five hours south in Brunswick, Doug McIntire was swallowing his third mug of black coffee as he watched the morning news, incredulous. He had joined Gustaf Adolph after moving to Aroostook County in the mid-1990s.

"I thought the church on the outside was beautiful, aside from the stucco," Doug recalled. "Inside the church, the Swedish style I found very gaudy; it's something that really has to grow on you—just all the fretwork and stuff, yuck. The wall-to-wall carpeting threw me; the pews are about as comfortable as a stone slab, and it was cold; it was really cold. I thought, *I'll just keep giving it a try.* The only other choice was my wife's church, and they're nuts, Seventh Day Adventists in Presque Isle. So I stuck it out and I kept going. And eventually some people started talking to me."

As time went on, Doug felt more and more welcome at the church, and even served on the council. In January 2003—three months before the poisoning—he returned to southern Maine to finish his schooling. Norma Bondeson replaced him on the council.

Doug had heard about the coffee episode earlier in the week and assumed it was a freak accident, probably involving a pesticide. He remembered having a problem with mice in his own home, and when he put out d-Con, those little buggers would take the pellets and stash them. So, he reasoned, that's probably what happened at the church. They put out some d-Con, and the mice had been sneaking the pellets into a seldom-used percolator, and someone then made coffee without first rinsing it out.

What he was hearing now, however, was something else entirely, and Doug was dumbfounded. As a councilor, Doug had become all too familiar with GA's politics and petty feuds. Still, this was over the top, even for GA. Someone had actually done this on purpose? He shook his head, thinking, *You people just couldn't stop fighting until someone got hurt, could you?*

"The shock and denial are all very fresh," a minister from a nearby church was telling *Good Morning America.*

"There hadn't been any kind of issues," a churchgoer said next. "We sit and discuss issues. We try to use common sense, and it just doesn't get heated, and it doesn't become big arguments."

What? Doug put down his mug as his jaw dropped. *It doesn't get heated? Ha! Who is this guy? He wasn't at the same GA I knew. Common sense? Right.*

As usual, Doug thought, *GA members were showing the outside world their shined-up veneer, not the snake pit underneath.* Still, almost any explanation would make more sense than murder by arsenic. Who would be capable of that?

"We expect somehow," the minister was saying, "as strange as it seems, it might be a member of the community."

At about noon Friday, Lt. Dennis Appleton gave the first of a series of news conferences that would help turn the New Sweden arsenic poisoning into a daily made-for-TV drama. Correspondents from all the major networks had flown into Presque Isle and Caribou. Reporters, photographers, producers, and satellite engineers were packing the Caribou Inn to full capacity, along with writers for the *Boston Globe*, the *Los Angeles Times*, and *People*. The *New York Times* had dubbed the poisoning "a real-life *Murder, She Wrote.*"

"I remember it being discussed on a morning conference call," said Larry Laughlin, executive editor for the

Northern New England Bureau of the Associated Press in Concord, New Hampshire. "Our Maine bureau chief, David Sharp, mentioned this thing going on up in New Sweden, where some people got sick at a church coffee. And I said, 'Where the hell's New Sweden?' And he said, 'Ah, it's just up north of Caribou.' And I remember saying, 'You mean there's something north of Caribou?'"

After thirty years in the news business, Laughlin knew a good story when he saw one, and he jumped on this one right away. "People being poisoned at a church coffee," he said. "That's really pretty neat—not one you get every week."

In Augusta, the Maine Department of Public Safety was deluged with calls from all over the world.

"It was the equivalent of 9/11," said Steve McCausland. "My top three stories, as far as news reaction goes, were New Sweden, 9/11/01, and 9/12/02—when the van went off into the Allagash."

McCausland was referring to the deadliest motor vehicle accident in Maine's history—when fourteen migrant workers were killed after their van veered off a one-lane bridge and into the Allagash River in the northern Maine wilderness.

"When that happened, my phone was ringing around the clock," he said. "New Sweden was equivalent to that."

At first, McCausland said, he tried to accommodate as many news outlets as possible.

"The commissioner went on CBS News one morning," he recalled. "It wasn't just a five-minute interview. The time factor included a pre-interview the day before, and two or three hours of lead time, getting him to (the local affiliate) WGME, setting up, and waiting there."

The next morning, McCausland said, the chief of the Maine State Police, Col. Michael Sperry, was scheduled to appear on another network news show. "Colonel Sperry stayed in Portland the night before, and then I got word that he had been preempted by some celebrity wedding. We had tried to accommodate them two or three times. And if you do one, you've gotta do them all. After the colonel was bumped, I made the decision it was nonproductive for our top people to be involved in all that down time. We had an investigation to run."

By Friday, the governor's office had issued an edict: Live media interviews were not to be granted. There would be no detectives, lieutenants, or any other state employees waxing on about the case with Katie Couric and Diane Sawyer.

Bill Stokes said that had it been up to him, the gag order would have gone even further. "I appreciate the edict," he said, "but my problem wasn't going on live TV—my problem was saying anything."

As Friday's news conference got under way, the front lawn of Caribou's courthouse resembled a soundstage, with state-of-the-art cameras, blinding white lights, silver umbrella reflectors, and snakelike extension cords crisscrossing the grass. The podium was a clutter of microphones flaunting giant, multicolored logos. Journalists gossiped, laughed, and exchanged theories and rumors about the poisoning. A photographer set his sturdy, eight-inch-high camera case behind the podium to serve as a riser. "Does that mean I'm too short?" Appleton said with a grin, stepping up. He looked at the cameras.

"Hello," he said, "I'm Lieutenant Dennis Appleton." He paused and squinted, scanning the crowd of reporters.

"Now I know a lot of you have been calling me, but if I returned all of your calls, I'd never get any investigating done."

"Lieutenant," a reporter called out, "we understand you found a container of arsenic in the church. Can you confirm that?"

Appleton paused. He looked first at the reporter, then out into the group.

"Straightening out misperceptions on the part of the press is like trying to get out of a muddy potato field in high gear."

His audience laughed. The show had begun.

Part Barney Fife, Part Columbo

Detective Mark Millett was one of the first investigators assigned to the New Sweden arsenic poisoning. Millett, a devoted family man with a devilish sense of humor, describes himself as "part Barney Fife, part Columbo." Tuesday night, two nights after the poisoning, he went to the home of Carl and Kristine Bondeson, who were members of Gustaf Adolph but had not attended Sunday's service. Their well-kept, ranch-style home was situated right on Route 161, a convenient and visible location for Down to Earth Gardens, Kristine's organic nursery.

Carl opened the door for the detective. "I've been expecting you," he said.

Millett was surprised. "Who told you I was coming?"

"Dan Rather," Carl replied with a grin. CBS, the only network with a signal reaching New Sweden, had just made the poisoning a national news story. "They said on TV that you were talking to all the members of the church."

The detective stepped inside, where Carl introduced him to Kristine and their son, Finn, who was lying on the couch watching TV. "He's sick," Kristine told the detective. "Would you like some coffee?"

"Sorry to hear you're under the weather," Millett said, smiling at the blond-haired boy. He looked pale. Millett turned to Kristine. "I'd love a cup," he said, "just black. Could we go into the kitchen and sit down?" Millett chatted with the couple, asking the same questions the police would ask every member of GA: Was anyone angry with you? Do you know of any arguments or grudges? Can you think of anyone who would want to kill you or other church members? All of the couple's answers were the same: "No."

As he put on his jacket to leave, Millett peered into the living room. "You'll start feeling better soon," he told Finn. "You probably can't wait to get back to school." The boy gave him a half-smile and went back to watching TV.

Millett reached into his breast pocket and pulled out two business cards. "Give me a call if anything comes up," he said, handing them to Carl and Kristine. "That number is good day and night." He shook Carl's hand and started toward the door, then stopped for a moment and slapped himself in the head.

"Oh, I almost forgot," he said. "May I speak to your son for just a minute?"

"Sure, but I don't think he'll be much help to you," Kristine said.

"How long has he been sick?" Millett asked.

"He spent the night with a friend last week," Kristine said, "and he came home sick. The doctor gave him a prescription, but it doesn't seem to have helped much."

"I won't keep him long," said Millett, turning toward the boy. He hiked up his trousers and sat in an armchair, leaning forward on his elbows. "So, Finn, when you're not playing sick, what do you do for fun?"

"I visit the farm where my pig lives," Finn replied, sitting up. "I have my own pig named Harriet. I won her in a pig scramble at the Presque Isle Fair."

"A pig scramble? Really?" Millett smiled. "And who lives at the farm besides Harriet?"

"Aunt Norma," the boy replied. "And guess what."

"What?"

"If we give Harriet a bowl of water, she knocks it over, and then she doesn't have any water all day. But if we give her two bowls of water, she knocks over one of them, and she keeps the other one to drink, so she has water all day long."

"Well, I'll be," the detective laughed. "I should try that with our puppy. Finn, did you go to church on Sunday?"

"No." The boy put his hand to his forehead and lay down. "Mom, my head hurts again."

This kid looks awful, Millett thought, but tried again: "Did anyone ask you to bring something to church on Sunday?

"No."

"Even as a joke, or to play a silly trick?"

Carl interrupted: "What exactly are you trying to say?"

"Mr. Bondeson, your son is very sick," Millett replied, standing up. "Don't you think you should have him checked for arsenic poisoning?"

Carl could hardly contain his fury. Was this fool accusing his son of being involved in what happened? "It's time for you to go," he said, showing the detective the door.

The following day Carl called the state police barracks in Houlton, where Millett was based. He was livid. "Don't send that guy back to this house," he said. "And I'd better not see him after dark."

Raindrops and Blood

Friday afternoon was damp and gray. A light sprinkle had started when Erica and her two sisters, Alicia and Kristi, left the hospital to have a late lunch. Erica and Alicia had been at Cary visiting Lois; Kristi worked in the lab and got off at three. Erica had cut her visit short because Friday was "Eureka night," when she would meet up with a group of friends at Eureka Hall in Stockholm. They would drink, kid around, and give each other a hard time. The three sisters went to Reno's, a fried-food joint in downtown Caribou, and finished up at half past four. Erica dropped Kristi and Alicia off at the hospital and headed home. She was ready to party.

On the way home Erica remembered there was no food in the house, and she pulled into Roy's IGA to get something quick for supper. The first person she saw was Butch, a grocery clerk. "Hey, Erica," he said, "I heard Bondeson shot himself because he's the one who poisoned your mom there."

"Butch, what are you talking about?" Erica stared at him. "Where the hell are you getting that from?"

"Some girl," Butch said with a shrug. "She come and stopped here to pick up something, and she told us that Danny was involved."

Erica got on her cell phone and called the hospital to tell her mother. It was the first Lois had heard of it. "I'll find out more and call you later," Erica told her, and hung up.

I'll call Debbie Blanchette, Erica thought, *even though I cannot stand the woman because she is as fake as fake comes—the biggest plastic faker there is. But she lives right in town and probably knows what's going on, so I'll call her anyway.* Erica dialed the number.

When her phone rang, Debbie was heading out the door to the New Sweden Town Office, right up Station Road from her home. State police had requested that all members of Gustaf Adolph come to the office to submit fingerprints, provide blood samples for DNA, and fill out questionnaires. There were four or five police cars at the office, and they suddenly squealed out of the parking lot and screeched past her house as she picked up the phone.

Erica sounded breathless. "Debbie, did something just happen? I heard there was a shooting on Bondeson Road. I don't know the whole story; have you heard anything?"

"A lot of sirens," Debbie replied. "I'll try to find out what's going on."

What now? Debbie thought. Only Danny Bondeson and two other families lived up there. Danny had graduated a couple of years ahead of her; she and his brother Carl had graduated together. He was the kind of guy she could call up and say, "Dad needs to have his roof shoveled. Can you come?" And he'd be there right away. He was easygoing, friendly, and always kind.

As Debbie sat in her kitchen, she recalled a recent conversation when a friend had remarked that whoever poisoned the church coffee was probably somebody no one would ever suspect. The realization struck her like thunder: It was Danny.

At the Bondeson farm, mayhem had erupted. Sirens blared, police cruisers screeched up, and an ambulance pulled into the driveway next to a tattered clapboard farmhouse. Rusted antique pickup trucks, wagon wheels, and machine parts were scattered about the property, and a canopy of treetops cast shadows on the lawn.

Debbie Blanchette was in her front yard listening to the commotion when Barbara Bondeson and her daughter Wanda came by.

"Is it Danny?" Debbie asked.

"They won't let us in," Barbara replied.

Debbie knew the Bondeson family had endured more than its share of losses in the last five or six years: young Paul's tragic accident; the sudden death of brother Pete; and exactly two years after that, Harold, the patriarch, passed away.

"Where is Norma?" Debbie asked Barbara.

"They won't let her in the house."

"Oh, my God, Barb," Debbie said. "Take care of Norma—just take care of Norma."

Detective Jim Hackett cautiously led investigators toward the craggy old house, semiautomatics close at hand. An ominous red trail lay before them—a few drops at first, then a pool. A long, gooey clot continued the path, and then—nothing. The ground was unstained for ten or fifteen feet, up to a wheelchair ramp that led to an enclosed porch. Hackett drew his gun, turned sideways, and slowly stepped inside. "Police!" he yelled. "We're coming in."

The farmhouse porch was cluttered with old lamps, stacks of books, and a hodgepodge of dusty furniture. Hackett waited for a moment, hearing no sound. On the floor just ahead he spotted a rifle, and next to it, a single live round of ammunition. At the threshold to the living room, a trail of wide, deep crimson splashes led to a sofa, its cushions soaked with blood.

Hackett motioned for the others to follow, and they entered the living room. Halfway into the kitchen a man was lying on the floor. He was wearing a down jacket with an enormous hole ripped open near the left shoulder. He was conscious, but bleeding heavily and breathing hard. Hackett leaned down and tried to talk to him. "What happened?"

The man gave him a look of contempt, closed his eyes, and turned his head away.

"I'm Carl Bondeson, his brother." Standing in the kitchen was a tall man with blond and gray hair. He said he had called 911. The man on the floor was his older brother Daniel, who lived at the farm.

The detectives looked at one another. Investigators had been in this same farmhouse the night before, interviewing Norma Bondeson. They had asked her who lived at the farm; she had mentioned only herself. Until this moment, the police had not been aware that Daniel Bondeson existed.

When the ambulance arrived, paramedics rushed in. Working calmly and quickly, they tried to stabilize Daniel as they loaded him onto a stretcher. "No, no," he was moaning, "just let me die." They carried him out, loaded him into the ambulance, climbed in, and slammed the door. The ambulance pulled out of the driveway and wailed its way to Caribou.

Out on the road, which had been cordoned off by police, Lt. Dennis Appleton was surrounded by reporters and photographers who had rushed to the Bondeson farm after getting word of a shooting. Appleton was removing his eyeglasses and pretending to weep in response to a reporter's complaint about missing her supper. "I've been eating Doritos," Appleton said, then winked at her and patted his belly. "It's not good for my cholesterol."

Dennis Appleton is a genial man with curly silver hair and an aw-shucks, folksy style. He came to Aroostook County late in his career, having raised a family in central Maine, before he was divorced and then later remarried. At fifty-three, he was the beaming dad of two-year-old Claire, and it didn't take much for him to pull out a wallet full of pictures.

Earlier in the day, Appleton had explained why police

believed the poisoning was deliberate. "We have done a lot of examination at the church," he said, "and we just can't see any evidence of an accident. There's no container there, no old pesticide container that was sitting in the cupboard." Also, he said, the concentration of arsenic was much too high for the poisoning to have been a mistake.

Now, just a few hours later, Appleton was again surrounded by reporters and photographers, this time in the cordoned-off road in front of the Bondeson farm. "We came here as a result of a report of an individual having been shot," he said. "That individual is a Donald, excuse me, Daniel Bondeson. He received a gunshot wound. He was transported to Cary Medical Center by ambulance; the last I heard he was in surgery there for a gunshot wound. I do not know his current condition."

First question: Was he a member of Gustaf Adolph?

"The Bondesons are members of the church," the lieutenant replied. "I do not know off the top of my head whether he was a real active member."

Appleton said police did not yet know if the shooting was self-inflicted. He did not believe Daniel Bondeson had been fingerprinted before the shooting; detectives had just set up their equipment at the town office when they were called out to the Bondeson farm. Police were now leaving the scene, but would return in the morning with a search warrant.

"And then, depending on what's happening, I may still try to do my noon briefing." Appleton's blue eyes crinkled up as he grinned: "I won't be able to contain all you people much longer than that."

Carl Bondeson needed to feed his cows, but he was afraid to go outside; there were too many reporters. Hackett agreed to go along with him; it would give them a chance to talk. The two men walked out to the barn, where Carl lifted the bar on the big metal latch. As the door creaked open, deep, hungry moos groaned out from the stalls, and a mix of earthy scents wafted through the air. "Yes, yes, I know, I know," Carl told his cows. "It's time for supper."

Carl led the way out into the big field and told Hackett he had been working at his family's greenhouse since about noon. His wife, Kristine, ran Down to Earth Gardens, marketing perennials, herbs, bushes, and shrubs to customers throughout the county and beyond. Today she had gone out to run errands, and Carl had been minding the store. At about 3 P.M., Carl said, he had a bad feeling, had driven to the Woodland farm, and found his wounded brother.

"What did you say to him?" the detective asked.

"I said, 'Why'd you do that? Why'd you do it?'" replied Carl.

"And what did he say?"

"He said, 'I felt like it.'"

"He felt like it?" Hackett paused. "Okay. And then?"

"I dialed 911."

"Any more conversation with your brother?"

"No," Carl replied. "That was it."

Oh sure, that's perfectly normal behavior, Hackett thought. "None whatsoever?"

"None," Carl said, watching a cow chomp on a mouthful of grass.

"Was your brother a member of Gustaf Adolph?"

"Yes," Carl replied. He walked back to the barn and held the door open for Hackett. They went inside, and Carl grabbed a large bucket and a shovel.

"Did he have something to do with the poisoning?"

"No," Carl said, looking straight at the cop. "Danny didn't do that, absolutely not." He went into a stall and began shoveling manure into the pail.

"How do you know?"

Carl stopped what he was doing and studied Hackett for a moment. "For starters, Danny's too stupid," he said, and resumed his work. "He couldn't pull that off even if he wanted to." Hackett watched as Carl went from stall to stall with his bucket and shovel. He emptied the pail into a large bin, put the shovel back against the wall, and rubbed his hands on his dungarees. He led Hackett back through the barn and closed the big door behind them. He fastened the latch and leaned against the door.

"Look," Carl said, "I'd tell Danny something simple, like, 'Go down and get me five bags of white potatoes.' He'd leave and come back with five potatoes, or a five-pound white bag, something like that. He couldn't get anything right. He couldn't even pour a glass of milk without spilling it."

As Carl told his story, the farm was crawling with cops. Uniformed troopers were stationed on the road to keep on-lookers away. Another officer walked the farm's perimeter, unwinding a roll of yellow tape with black lettering: CRIME SCENE: DO NOT ENTER. Out behind the barn, three detectives were walking toward the chicken coop when they noticed several objects on the ground: a pen, some feathers, and a baseball cap.

The door to the chicken coop was open, and Detective Lloyd Deschaine went inside. A spent rifle shell lay on the floor. There were feathers everywhere. *Of course there are feathers*, he thought, *it's a chicken coop*. He walked back and forth, bent over, picked up a feather and rubbed it between his thumb and forefinger. It was small and very soft. Wait a minute, Deschaine thought, these feathers are down. They came from the jacket of the guy on the floor.

In the kitchen, Detective Mark Millett spotted something on the table. Nobody had noticed it before. Among the papers, dirty glasses, and crumbs of old food was a note, dampened by raindrops and splashed with blood. He picked it up.

"Hey," Millett called out, "look what I found."

An Odd Little Duck

As Daniel Bondeson lay hemorrhaging on a surgical table at Cary Medical Center, Detective Mark Millett arrived at the Caribou Nursing Home, a single-story brick building spread out on a hilltop above downtown Caribou. He got out of his cruiser and walked through the front entrance into a clean, tastefully furnished reception area.

"Good evening," he said to a woman sitting at the front desk. He showed her his badge. "Detective Mark Millett from Maine State Police. Does Daniel Bondeson work here?"

"Yes," she replied, appearing slightly surprised. "He works on D. Go straight down that hallway and turn right."

Since 2001, Daniel Bondeson had been working at the nursing home as a CNA—certified nurse's aide. His job was to bathe, dress, and feed people who were either too sick or too old to care for themselves. Daniel was a dependable employee, always prompt and willing to come in on short notice. So when he didn't show up for his three-to-eleven shift on Friday, May 2, the staff became concerned. "The scheduler called his house," coworker Lori Poisson said later, "and a person who answered the phone said he couldn't come to the phone, but they would give him a message."

Millett wandered through the hallway, grimacing at the antiseptic yet slightly rotten scent that permeated the hallway. Most of the residents were in wheelchairs, their heads bobbing like dolls in trinket shops. *Shoot me if I ever end up here*, he thought to himself. *I'd rather be dead than stinking up diapers and drooling. Even if Bondeson didn't shoot himself, he probably wanted to after a couple of years of this place.*

In a minute or two he reached a nursing station. A woman in a tidy white uniform was writing on a chart. "Is this D wing?" Millett asked her.

"Yes. May I help you?"

He took out his badge.

"Detective Mark Millett, Maine State Police."

"Oh!" The nurse looked alarmed. "I'm Diana Gandee. Is something wrong?"

"Is there someplace we can talk in private?"

"Follow me," she said, and showed Millett to an office just beyond the nursing station. "Sherry?" she said, peeking into the door. "There is a detective here from the Maine State Police."

"A detective? Lord. Bring him in."

The nurse stepped into the office and gestured to Millett. "Detective Millett, this is our supervisor, Sherry Parker." She gestured toward another nurse sitting in the office. "And this is Maggie Evans."

"Glad to meet you both," Millett said. "May I sit down?"

"Of course," the supervisor replied.

"There's been an accident," Millett told her, pulling up a chair. "Daniel Bondeson has been shot. It appears to have been self-inflicted, but we aren't sure yet."

"Shot?" The women stared at Millett. "Is he dead?"

"He's in surgery at Cary—no word yet on his condition. Do you mind if I ask you a few questions?"

"No," Sherry replied, blinking. "Go ahead."

"Is there any arsenic here?" Millett asked. "I mean, is arsenic used for anything at all in the facility?"

"Arsenic?" The nurse looked perplexed. "No, we don't have any arsenic here."

"What can you tell me about Daniel Bondeson?"

The nurses were quiet.

"Did you notice anything unusual about his behavior recently, anything at all?"

Diana spoke up. "Danny's the wallflower," she said. "He spends most of the time by himself, kind of does his own thing."

"Has he been unusually quiet recently?" the detective asked.

"That's how he always is," Diana said, shrugging.

"Wait a minute," Maggie said. "I did notice on Wednesday night that he was different. He didn't speak to anybody that night. In fact, we all commented on it, that he was so quiet." She looked at Diana. "Remember? We were talking about that during break." Maggie looked back at Millett. "He wasn't one to chitchat or anything like that, but that night he was completely silent. The other weird thing about that week—he got a couple of phone calls, which never happened before. Nobody ever called Danny. But one night a man called late in his shift. I don't know which night it was, but it was after the poisoning. I have no idea who it was; he just asked to speak to Daniel Bondeson. That was the first call I'd ever seen him get."

Millett was jotting things down in a small spiral notebook. "What else can you tell me about him?"

"Two nights ago he made a telephone call," Diana said. "He called some lady in New Sweden. He asked her if she had watched the news and if they found out who had done the poisoning at the church."

"Really," the detective said. "Do you know who the woman was?"

"No," Diana replied. "I didn't catch her name."

"What is he like?" Millett asked.

"He's weird," Maggie said. "He asks questions that show no common sense. Simple little things that he should know before coming on the floor, like 'How do you take a temperature?' Stupid things like that. We think maybe he's a lot smarter than we are; he's telling us he don't know how to do it so we'll do it for him. I think he really knows what the answers are. He's a slacker."

"He's lazy," Diana added. "At mealtimes, he'll be leaning against the wall, and he'll say something like, 'Who am I supposed to feed? I'm waiting for the food carts.' You have to help other people in this job, and that's not a strong suit for him, helping others."

"You can say anything to him and it goes right over his head," Maggie said. "I mean, nobody intentionally wants to hurt his feelings, but sometimes we'll tease him, say something like, 'Let's go out tonight, Dan, where are all those credit cards?' And he'll say, 'They're in my back pocket.' He'll go along with it. He's just an odd little duck."

"He's been spoken to about body odor at least twice," Diana added. "He is kind of an oddball, but not in a bad way. He has a gentle demeanor."

"Do you think he had something to do with the poisoning at that church?" Maggie asked.

"Do you?" Millett asked.

"Personally, I don't think he has the guts to do it," Maggie replied, "and I don't think he's bright enough to do it." She was quiet for a moment. "Did he do it?"

"We don't know yet," Millett said. "Possibly."

There was silence for a moment before Maggie spoke: "I still don't think he'd have enough smarts to put that whole thing together. If he did it, then someone else did all the planning, and he was just the follower."

Erica left the Caribou IGA and drove seven or eight miles to Northstar Variety, New Sweden's only gas station and convenience store. In fact, it was New Sweden's only store, and the proprietors, Sara and Dave Anderson, managed to stock their small space with a wide selection of supplies—from sugar to snowshoes to sweatshirts. It also served as a tagging station during hunting season, and there was plenty of hot, fresh coffee for the locals who stopped by in pickup trucks for a newspaper, a tank of gas, or a pickled egg. Northstar wasn't Wal-Mart, but it sure beat driving to Presque Isle for a fishing lure.

It was also gossip central. Erica fidgeted impatiently while a journalist from New York interviewed Sara. She would get the real dirt only after he left.

"What's going on?" she asked Sara as the door closed behind the reporter.

"There's been a shooting at the Bondesons'," Sara told her. "It was Danny. He's still alive; the ambulance took him to Caribou."

Sara had heard this from her husband, Dave, who had been walking near the farm when the chaos broke out and had gone over to see what it was about. He noticed a car parked in front of the farm with several people inside, including Norma Bondeson. As Dave leaned down to look at her, she snapped, "What do you know about this?"

"I'm just here looking for a moose to take pictures of," he had replied.

"She was unnerved," Dave said later. "It was like she was worried I knew something."

On her way out of the store, Erica bumped into an acquaintance. "Hey," he said, "Danny Bondeson just shot himself."

"I know. I've known since it first happened," Erica said.

"It was in the chest," he told her.

Now wait a minute, Erica thought. *I had a best friend that killed himself, and it's automatic with guys; they go right to the head. I've researched it—guys do not shoot themselves in the chest. This guy is full of shit. He's a bullshitter anyway.*

"See you later," Erica said, and went on her way.

. . .

Bill Stokes was sitting at his desk in the Attorney General's office on Friday evening when the call came in about Daniel Bondeson's shooting.

"I was sitting right here," Stokes said, "and I had actually made a remark to Dennis earlier in the week—I'd said, 'Dennis, I'll bet you'll solve this in a week'—jokingly. I was sitting here late in the afternoon when the call came in that he had been shot, and there was a note that was found. We didn't know much about it, but it looked as though he had taken responsibility or expressed some responsibility, and he was going to survive. That was the expectation, and that is what was told to me—that they expected him to survive. And I left that night thinking he was going to survive. We talked about, okay, how are we going to interview him, search warrants, the house, and plans for interviewing him when he was able. We talked about that."

Stokes left the office and drove home, feeling lucky that the attempted suicide had failed. If Bondeson had admitted to the poisoning in a note, perhaps they could get a confession. This could be a nice break.

Stokes would have no such luck. At Cary Medical Center, the efforts of surgeons to save Daniel Bondeson failed, and at 6 P.M. on Friday he was pronounced dead. Reporters got word of his passing in time for the eleven o'clock news, but much to his irritation, Stokes was never notified.

"I got up at five o'clock in the morning and saw the paper," Stokes recalled. "So that's how I knew. I wasn't happy about that, either."

Sperry Takes the Stage

Detectives descended on the Bondeson farm with a search warrant early Saturday morning with two objectives: to figure out who shot Daniel Bondeson, and to find a link to the poisoning at the church. For several hours, the normally isolated road was teeming with journalists from all over the country trying to get as close to the farm as possible without crossing either the cops or the yellow crime-scene tape. Shortly before noon, the detectives left the farm and headed back to the Caribou courthouse for a media briefing.

The chief of the Maine State Police, Col. Michael Sperry, had been flown from Augusta to Caribou to conduct the briefing, which was to air live on CNN. This was unprecedented; never before had CNN broadcast a live report from Maine.

On the courthouse lawn, the crowd of journalists and technical people was even larger than the day before. Two extraordinary events had occurred—first a fatal poisoning and now a deadly shooting—in a town with a crime rate normally close to zero. It seemed a likely guess that the incidents were connected, but among the media, nobody knew for sure.

A hush fell over the group as a tall figure appeared and strode toward the microphones.

If Dennis Appleton was Wilford Brimley, then Mike Sperry was Harrison Ford. Dressed in his steel-blue trooper's uniform and a wide-brimmed, tasseled hat, Colonel Sperry cut a striking figure as he took his place at the podium.

"Yesterday, as many of you have reported, our troopers were called to the scene of a shooting in Woodland," Sperry began. He paused for a moment, letting the journalists hang on his words. "As a result of that," he continued, "we have developed information which links that shooting to the death at the church, and the poisoning of the people who are in the hospital."

Questions started flying. "Was the shooting a suicide?"

"This was reported as a self-inflicted gunshot wound. We're still investigating that."

"Can you tell us what the link is?"

"It's too early to provide that information at this time."

"So you're no longer looking for suspects?"

"That's not true. This is an open investigation."

"Sir, did he leave a note?"

"I wouldn't comment on a note at this time, but we do have information that would link him to the poisonings at the church."

"Have you established a motive?"

"We have developed information in the last twenty-four hours that would indicate what the motive might have been."

"Did Daniel Bondeson put the arsenic in the coffee?"

"It's too early to make a determination on that."

"Sounds like you've got this case ninety-five to ninety-eight percent cinched up," a reporter said. "Is that a fair assessment?"

"After twenty-six years of police work," Sperry said, "I would tend to think the real work is just starting."

"Were any members of the Bondeson family at church that day? Did they drink the coffee?"

"To my knowledge, no members of the Bondeson family had coffee that day or were ill."

"Have you been able to locate his sister?" Suspicions about Norma Bondeson had been whispered to the press already.

"We have talked with other family members," Sperry replied.

"Are there other suspects?"

"We could not rule out that there are other suspects at this time. Thank you." Sperry turned away from the microphones and disappeared before the reporters could stop him.

Origins

To those who had known Daniel Bondeson all his life, the notion that he would maliciously poison the church congregation was ridiculous. Even the most dogged reporters could not find a single soul who said that Daniel was capable of deliberate harm.

"Nobody in this world can convince me that he did it himself; I never will believe that," said Omar Lagasse, a member of Gustaf Adolph for thirty-seven years. A devout Christian, Omar hangs tapestries of Jesus on his bedroom walls, and he prays for every single soul he meets. He belongs to a Pentecostal church, having left GA after Pastor Scottie Burkhalter's final service on Easter 2001.

Omar thought the world of Daniel Bondeson. "He came here one Sunday afternoon and shoveled my roof. And I asked him how much he wanted, and he said, 'Give me what you want.' I had been paying forty dollars, so I gave him forty bucks. He held it in his hand; he looked at me and said, 'Omar, do you have any money to buy groceries?' I said, 'Yes, why?' He said, 'If you didn't have any money to buy groceries, I'd give you back your money and you can go buy groceries, and I'd do this job for nothing. Anything you want done around here, I'll do it for nothing.' This was just a week before this happened. Does that sound like a man who could—never, never. No matter how hard you try to convince me, you can give me a million dollars to believe it; you can give me two. You can give me any amount you want; I still say he didn't do that. I know him well enough for that."

Omar was asked if someone else might have put Danny up to it. "I have my ideas," he replied, "but I like to keep them to myself."

The suggestion that Daniel would shoot himself also perplexed many of those who remembered him as a physical fitness buff with the considerable enthusiasm and fortitude required to complete the Boston Marathon three times. There were others, however, who had noticed he was beginning to fray around the edges.

"Danny was an avid runner," said Eldredge Palmer, a retired social studies teacher and long-distance runner. "One year he went out to Eugene, Oregon, which was the hotbed of distance running in the United States at that time. And he was out there for a few months, and he trained out there, and when he came back, he was real good.

"I've got pictures of some of the races with me and Danny. Some of them, we're standing with our trophies after the race. There was one in Limestone, Fourth of July—my wife took pictures of us. There's a lot of runners up here; we used to travel around quite a bit, downstate and different areas, and he used to be there. We didn't go together, but I used to see him there, and we were friendly with each other."

Over the past several years, however, Danny had been running less and less.

"His complaint was he had to work so hard there on the farm that he didn't have the energy and the time to run the mileage that the rest of us did," said Eldredge. "Of course, distance running is how well you race, how hard you can train, and how many miles you can put in. Well, it's hard to be on your feet and working hard all day and do that. I found standing up teaching school all day was hard on my legs."

Although his running had fallen off in recent years, Danny continued to log hundreds of miles on cross-country skis and had won some impressive races: the Vasaloppet in Sweden, twice, and the American Birkebeiner in Wisconsin. At home, he had organized and directed the local Winter's End Ski Touring Race.

Genealogy was also his passion. In 1968, at age eighteen, Danny penned the history of his family. The project was a school homework assignment, but it may have helped to inspire Daniel's lifelong dedication to his Swedish heritage. Over the years he had served as president of the Woodland Historical Society, which his mother had helped to establish, and he volunteered as caretaker of its two buildings, a one-room schoolhouse and a historic home. Daniel mowed the lawn, shoveled snow from the roof, and worked the door on Sundays during the spring and summer, when the tiny museum was open to the public. He was also active in the restoration of the historic walking-trail system used by his own ancestors when they emigrated from Sweden in the late nineteenth century, and occasionally he attended Swedish Club meetings, where local Swedes would congregate to share stories about their heritage. "He definitely was Swedish," said Eldredge, "he definitely was Swedish. They all have the same mind-set, so to speak. Their heritage means everything to them."

Every year out in the big barn, Dan helped his sister Norma and his brother Carl create floral oat sheaves, a Swedish holiday decoration, which Norma then sold wholesale to large companies such as L.L. Bean, and at gift shows in big cities such as Boston and Philadelphia. "Some people probably thought the Bondesons were a little foolish," said Jerry Nelson, an old family friend. "They were harvesting their grain with the old-fashioned binder, and did it like they did fifty or a hundred years ago. But they did it because that's the way they sold their sheaves."

In the mid-1990s Daniel wrote a series of colorful letters to a cousin by marriage, Carol Bondeson, recounting detailed and humorous stories about the Bondeson clan. In one such letter, dated November 20, 1994, Daniel remembered a Sunday visit with Harold, his father, to the home of Great-Aunt Mathilde, or "Thilda." Harold had brought along a bottle of beer, and "Thilda said he shouldn't drink it, took it from him, and poured it into a glass jar," Daniel wrote. "She then took a sip, put the cover on the jar, and put it in the cupboard."[1] Daniel took his father on many such outings, dropping in on long-lost relatives throughout Aroostook County, and writing about them in letters to distant family members throughout the United States and Sweden.

In June 1995, Daniel flew to Sweden to compete in the Stockholm Marathon. While there he visited with a cousin, Nils Truedsson, who took him to a farm in the south, where the Bondeson family had roots.[2] The clan had been on the Hasslekarr farm since at least the 1770s, and it was with the birth of a boy named Mans in 1834 that the surname Bondesson came about. Swedish peasants had begun to use a patronymic system, whereby the child's last name was determined by the father's first name. Mans was Bonde's son—Bondesson—and the second "s" was dropped when Mans later immigrated to America. When his own children were born, Mans adopted the American tradition of naming, and thus the Bondeson name was perpetuated.[3]

Sweden made Lutheranism the official state religion in 1527, and the country was divided into parishes. Mans was listed in parish records as a "separatist—religious dissenter."[4] Such people were treated harshly in nineteenth-century Sweden. They were subjected to ridicule, harassment, and even jail for petty offenses. In fact, the persecution of non-Lutherans is believed to be a major reason why Mans left Sweden for America in April 1871.[5]

There were other incentives as well. In 1860, the United States Census had revealed that while other states were growing, Maine was not. In 1862, William Widgery Thomas,

Jr., a Maine native, was appointed American Consul to Sweden by President Abraham Lincoln. At the port of Goteberg, Thomas witnessed shiploads of Swedes leaving for America and thought, *What better place than Maine for these hardy folks to settle?* Thomas returned to Maine and successfully launched an effort to establish a Swedish colony. Legislation was passed to provide the head of each Swedish family with a one-hundred-acre lot, to be exempt from property taxes for five years. In return, each lot holder was to clear at least fifteen acres and put the land to use. If after five years these conditions were met, the settlers were given the deed to their property.[6]

In March 1870, Governor Joshua Chamberlain appointed Thomas commissioner of the newly created Maine Board of Immigration, and he headed back to Sweden to begin recruiting. By June 1870, fifty-one Swedes had arrived in Maine, having paid their own steamship passage and carrying a "certificate of character." One month later, on July 23, 1870, they founded the town of New Sweden.[7]

Mans Bondeson and his wife, Bengta, Daniel's great-grandparents, were among those first fifty-one settlers. They sailed across the North Sea to Leith, Scotland, took a train to Glasgow, then rode a steamship across the Atlantic Ocean. According to a 1985 family history handwritten by Daniel's mother, Thorborg, during this phase of the trip Bengta gave birth to a son, Nels. The captain of the ship and his wife offered the Bondesons one thousand dollars—then a king's ransom—for the infant, but Mans and Bengta declined. To this day, visitors to the Fairview Cemetery in Perham, Maine, can see the words "Born on the High Seas" inscribed on Nels's headstone.[8]

After eighteen days at sea, the Bondesons arrived in Halifax, Nova Scotia, then crossed the Bay of Fundy to New Brunswick. They took a boat to Woodstock and another boat up the Aroostook River to Fort Fairfield, Maine. The family of three arrived in New Sweden by wagon on June 4, 1871.[9]

Over the next seven years Mans and Bengta would have

four more children: Sven (Daniel Bondeson's grandfather), Aaron, Annie, and Alice. In 1893, Mans decided his lot was too swampy, and he purchased the farm in Woodland.[10] That is the place where Daniel Sven Bondeson would spend his entire life, and where, in 2003, his violent death would become the focus of Maine's most famous homicide.

ENDNOTES

1. Carol Bondeson, *The Origin of the Bondeson Family in Maine* (Carol and Roger Bondeson, 1995), p. 38.
2. Ibid., p. 11.
3. Ibid., p. 11.
4. Ibid., p. 13.
5. Ibid., p. 15.
6. Ibid., p. 14.
7. Ibid., p. 14.
8. Ibid., p. 18.
9. Ibid., p. 18.
10. Ibid., p. 25.

Danny Boy

Sunday, May 4, was another sunny, cool morning. Members of Gustaf Adolph were gathering for the first time since the poisoning, and two other local congregations, Covenant and Trinity, joined them in support and sympathy. A phalanx of television cameras and scribbling reporters lined the street as stoic Swedes with names like Erickson, Peterson, and Olson filed into the old sanctuary, pausing occasionally for a nod and a whisper of comfort. Suspicion and sadness filled the pews, wearing their Sunday finest.

Governor Baldacci arrived in a plain blue sedan, stepped out, and spotted the cameras as quick as a cat smells tuna. He straightened the jacket of his neat, dark blue suit, paused for a moment, and, always in frame, smiled. Slowly crossing the lawn, he offered gentle handshakes to a scattering of churchgoers; then, smoothing his jacket, he strode inside.

Staff members of Cary Medical Center arrived and were seated. Journalists hovered in the back of the church, where they had been ordered to stand along the wall. Two or three went upstairs and sat in the balcony. The reporters didn't pretend to be mourning or praying; some flipped through Bibles or hymnals; others just watched and took notes. A spirited, pressure-cooker atmosphere had been heating up among them for days. Local reporters felt outgunned on their own turf by network big shots.

Standing at the front door was Sven Bondeson, Danny's nephew. Sven's father, Peter, was Danny's brother; he had died three years earlier when an aneurysm burst in an artery near his stomach. Now Sven was nervously waiting for Erica, who had promised to sit with him. He wanted to attend the service but felt somewhat uncomfortable, fearing people might be angry with the Bondesons. Erica was true to her word, and when she arrived, the two went upstairs, where several reporters were already seated. "Do you think they have any idea who we are?" Sven whispered as he and Erica sat in the last row.

"Who cares?" Erica said. "I'm not ashamed to tell them, either."

Only one media outlet, the *Bangor Daily News*, was permitted to take photographs inside the church. "Alicia had it out with the *Bangor Daily News*," Erica said later. "They took pictures of her crying."

Down in the sanctuary, state police detectives stood to the side, studying faces, watching movements. The garage-style doors to the fellowship hall were rolled open, keeping the coffeepot, which was guarded by two state troopers, clearly in view.

In a middle pew, Beth Salisbury sat beside her grandparents. She had served on the church council until right before the poisoning, and when it happened she decided to quit. *Crazy fucking people*, she thought, *there's so much inbreeding up here they can't think straight. I should've stayed in New York. I come up here expecting it to be relaxed and serene and comfortable. Now someone did this horrible thing, and we don't know when or where they'll do it again, if they're gonna show up at the school or what.*

Poor Reid, she thought, *he would be the last person anyone would want to hurt. He was so funny!* At council meetings he'd sit across from Beth just to tease her. "I need someone beautiful to look at," he'd say. One time he saw her fixing Cassie's hair, and he'd come over and messed Beth's all up. *God, I'll miss him*, she thought.

Beth knew she'd had a narrow escape. Last Sunday had been her sixteenth wedding anniversary. She and Brett had planned to take the kids to church, but the children had stopped them. "Happy anniversary," Cassie had said. "We're making you breakfast in bed." *Oh, my God*, Beth thought now, *if anything happened to Brett I don't know what I'd do. And God forbid one of my kids. How could someone do something so evil, especially in the house of God?*

"Be with us in this time of fear and violation, anxiety and suspicion," prayed Associate Bishop Hans Arneson. "Strengthen our resolve to love our neighbor."

"Love our neighbor"—my ass, thought Beth. *I'll never set foot in this church again, and neither will my kids. Jesus Christ, if it weren't for Nana and Pop, we wouldn't even have come here today.*

"We are afflicted in every way, but not crushed; perplexed, but not in despair." Bishop Margaret Payne, head of the New England Evangelical Lutheran Church Synod, was reading from her notes. "Struck down—but not destroyed."

Not destroyed, perhaps, but certainly heartbroken. Two lifelong members of the tiny congregation were dead, the circumstances inconceivable. Beth watched as old, familiar faces walked through the door. *Some of them would give you the shirt off their back*, she thought, *others would steal it in a heartbeat.*

For the rest of the congregation, losing Reid was devastating enough. But the idea that Danny—full-blooded Swede, one of their own—might have committed this terrible deed was unbearable. No, they thought, it couldn't be the Danny we've known all his life, whose mother would come to church with Norma, Peter, and Becky, and the little boys, Danny, Carl, and Paul. Thorborg would bring

them in, and guess what—they behaved. They were just little, tiny bits of things.

White-haired women took hankies from their pocket-
books. "How Great Thou Art" was punctuated with sobs,
but it was the Hymn of the Day that raised goose bumps on
some and caused startled heads to turn. The melody was
familiar; the organist played it powerfully; no one sang the
lyrics.

Don Peters, who had come to pray for his old friend
Ralph Ostlund, was a musician, and had heard this song for
as long as he could remember. Don looked around him and
saw no reaction. He turned his head and locked eyes with a
reporter sitting behind him. " 'Danny Boy!' " he exclaimed
in a whisper. "Yes!" the reporter replied. They stared at one
another.

The sad, lovely strains poured from the organ in waves
of love and forgiveness, with words not sung, but felt: Oh
Danny boy, we love you so, our Danny boy. You were a part
of our church family. We'll miss you so. Oh Danny boy,
we'll miss you so.

It was a tribute fit for the heavens.

After the service, the reporter found the organist and
complimented her on the selection. The organist looked
perplexed. She didn't even know "Danny Boy." The Hymn
of the Day was "O Christ the Same," and it had been cho-
sen a month earlier. That the song shared its melody with
an old Irish ballad was purely a coincidence.

Outside, several dozen media crews were vying for the
best spots in front of the podium, which had been set up for
the bishop, the governor, and the commissioner of public
safety. Standing behind them were Ed Margeson, Janet Erickson, and Erica Grace Anderson, each of whom would
speak on behalf of the church.

"I'd like to call your attention to the fact that I'm enjoying a cup of coffee," Bishop Payne said, smiling broadly as
she raised a cup and drank. "We are here today to reclaim
this space as a place of worship and a place of healing. It's

important for everyone to know that this still is a place where we get together in worship and in safety."

A reporter asked Janet Erickson if returning to church had frightened her. "I'm not afraid," Janet replied. "It was good to be in there. This is the place we need to pray, to all be together and worship God."

How were people reacting to the danger? "There is forgiveness and love," Janet said. Erica nodded vigorously behind her. "Because everybody loves everybody."

Will the Bondeson family be alienated because of this? Erica shook her head while Janet spoke again: "I don't think so. I certainly hope not."

Ed Margeson, whose thirty-year-old son, Erich, was the youngest to be poisoned, spoke about their "close-knit community."

"I hope what you see here this morning is an example of how close we are," he said. "Perhaps as a community, we've lost a bit of our innocence."

It was Erica's turn. "As far as I'm concerned, we are all family," she said. "We are a great community; all in all, everybody knows everybody, we have great traditions we practice." She suddenly appeared flustered. "We—and— like I said—"

"Let me butt in for just a second," Governor Baldacci said, stepping forward. Erica moved aside. "I think the great message is, you see how the whole community is pulling together in spite of the tragedy. It shows that resilience, that Aroostook County resilience."

Later, Governor Baldacci was driven to Cary Medical Center. "He visited my mother," Erica said, beaming. "He told my mother that he thought I was a great person and a great speaker."

Michael Cantara, Maine's new commissioner of public safety, was the last person to address the media. "The work that has been performed by local and state officials in solving this incident has been remarkable," he said. "The coordination has been top-notch." Someone stepped up and whispered in Cantara's ear. The "incident," the commissioner was reminded, had not yet been solved.

After the service, Lt. Dennis Appleton met with reporters. Was there reason to believe that the poisoner was still on the loose? "I would say yes," he replied. "There's a reason to believe that. We have not made any arrests in the case."

Watching the news at home that evening, Bill Stokes was already becoming irritated. *Why do they keep talking about this?* he wondered.

"It's not the way I operate," he said later. "There was an atmosphere of 'Let's keep talking! It's Poisoning Central! Let's keep talking!' It's just not the way I operate."

To the people of New Sweden, the media onslaught felt like an infestation of Maine black flies. "It was bad," Debbie Blanchette recalled. "There were hordes; so many, so many everywhere. People would be interviewed down at Sara's store, and somebody would come out, somebody who probably hadn't been to church for ages, and they were interviewing them. The rest of us just gathered together, and we wanted to say, 'Stay out, everybody who doesn't belong. This is our church family, and just leave us alone.' And you'd see these news trucks, and reporters coming out of the store and talking to people, and we're thinking, *Why?* This is our church, and so why are you talking about Danny if you don't really know him? He belongs to us and not to you. None of us would talk."

Meatballs and Magic

Detective Lloyd Deschaine pulled out a chair in the inter-view room at the Criminal Investigation Division of the Maine Department of Public Safety. He sat down at the large rectangular wooden table, which was dotted with deep, black cigarette burns. Deschaine smoked Camels, but now everything was smoke-free this and smoke-free that, so the butts had to stay in his pocket. As for the cigarette burns, Deschaine could recite exactly which one went with what case. That gay fellow who got tossed off the bridge, right here; the pot dealer buried alive, right over there; and the little girl starved by her demon-crazy mom, that one right there.

Three other detectives—Jim Hackett, Mark Millett, and Frank Bechard—were seated around the table watching as Deschaine's stubby yellow pencil scratched across a white legal pad, sketching the Bondeson farm. Deschaine was the lead detective on the New Sweden arsenic poisoning, and he was talking about Daniel. "So he's clear over here," De-schaine said, looking up. "Shoots himself—bam. But uh-oh, he's not dead." He looked down at his pad and drew a stick figure. "He's got another bullet in his hand. It's rain-ing. The raindrops are hitting the note; it's getting kind of wet, so he says, 'I'm gonna pick up my note, and I'm going back inside.'" Deschaine drew an unsteady line from the chicken coop to the house. "So he's going back; he's at the ramp, drops the gun and the bullet, drops it there, lies down on the couch, gets back up, then falls down and collapses in the kitchen."

Deschaine sat back in his chair and stuck the pencil be-hind his ear. "We should've gotten smallpox vaccinations before going inside that dump," he said, folding his arms. "Nothing's been thrown out in fifty fuckin' years."

He was just about right. Inside the Bondeson farm-house, ceiling-high stacks of newspapers formed a maze so narrow that the cops had to walk through it sideways. In the front bedroom, a tattered pair of men's brown shoes re-mained next to the bed where old Harold had died. In an-other room was a mattress covered with grimy sheets and a soiled old sleeping bag. Next to it was a bucket of urine. That was Danny's room.

"Okay, Hackett, whaddya got?" Deschaine said, sitting up. "You talked to Carl?"

"Yeah, I talked to him." Hackett pulled out a pocket-sized blue spiral notebook and opened it.

"Hey, Hack," Millett interrupted, "before you start—have you bonked that ugly reporter yet?"

"I resent your calling her that," Hackett replied. "In the future, Millett, please refer to her as 'that horny reporter.'" He snickered. "And it won't take me long—she's been lookin' for love in all the wrong places and seems very ea-ger to please. I'll keep you posted on that."

"Eager to please? I like that quality in a woman," Millett said. "I have found that looks aren't everything—it's what's inside that counts." He pointed toward his lap. "Send her right this way."

"Hackett!" Deschaine barked. "What about Carl?"

Hackett sat upright and cleared his throat. "Okay, here goes: Carl says Friday morning the three of them—Carl,

Norma, and Danny—were at the house. Carl and Norma are sitting at the table, and Norma's saying, 'The cops were here. They suspect me; they think I did it.' A couple of feet away, Danny's lying on a couch in the living room, not really joining in the conversation. He's just lying there, taking it in, but not saying a word. So Carl says, 'I gotta go. It's quarter to twelve, and I need to go watch the greenhouse; Kristine's got to go to town. See you later.' So Carl leaves. He's got to be at the greenhouse by twelve, so he takes off. Then Norma takes off. She's going to that funeral—Hazel somebody—wait, here it is—Hazel Lindgren, in Caribou.

"A couple of hours later, Carl goes back up to the farm—supposedly because he had a 'bad feeling.' So I told him, point blank, I said, 'Somebody called you to come back up there, they must have.' And he said no and then told me another story about having the same bad feeling before, and he acted on it, and something bad happened. He said it was a premonition."

"Oh, so now he's psychic?" Deschaine chuckled.

"You know those Swedes, famous for meatballs and magic." Millett sighed.

"Right," Bechard agreed, "and the church coffee was a witch's brew."

"So that would explain the toad's head and vulture's wing in the pot," added Millett.

"Okay, okay." Deschaine sighed. "Keep going, Hackett. Carl had a premonition. What else?"

"All right, another thing," Hackett said. "Carl was in charge of the greenhouse while his wife was gone. When she gets home, she comes in and the door's open; nobody's in the greenhouse. Nobody's watching it. She goes in the house, nobody's there, and she's wondering, where's Carl?"

"He ran out of there like a bat out of hell," Deschaine said.

"That's right," Hackett said, nodding. "Somebody must have called him."

"Danny?" Millett suggested. "Danny might have called

and said, 'I'm gonna blow myself away,' and Carl would have rushed right over there."

"True, but why wouldn't Carl just tell us that?" Hackett said.

Bechard held up a hand. "Hold it a second. Do we believe this was suicide or not?"

"Not a hundred percent," Deschaine said. "He was shot in the chest. It'll be interesting to see that autopsy report."

"If he really wanted to die," Millett said, "why didn't he just have a cup of that nice church coffee?"

"Millett, when you retire, you really ought to take the comedy routine on the road," Deschaine yawned. "But till then, give it a rest, will ya? I'd like to get outta here before midnight. Bechard, what about our friend Norma? You say she went to a funeral somewhere?"

"Hazel Lindgren's in Caribou," Bechard replied. "I checked. Norma was there. She signed in—people saw her there. We measured the time it would've taken her to get from the farm to the funeral and back to the farm. She could have done it—but only if she ran into the funeral parlor, said, 'So long, Hazel, nice knowing you,' and bolted right back out again. What—so she could go home, shoot her brother, and still have an alibi?"

"Yeah, all right," Deschaine said, and looked over at Millett. "So let's hear about the note."

"It's bogus, if you ask me." Millett grunted. "The material is canned. But hey, not everyone thinks so." Millett glanced at his wristwatch. "What were you saying about staying here till midnight?"

"Be here at 8 A.M.," Deschaine said, standing up. "Bring doughnuts. And Hackett—when your fly is open, keep your mouth shut. Remember that when you see your horny reporter."

Bad Blood

By Monday, May 5, the New Sweden community was reeling with disbelief, having spent the previous eight days coping with the country's largest-ever deliberate arsenic poisoning, a media invasion that had turned their town into a nightly television drama, and now, the shooting death of native son Daniel Bondeson. Over the weekend Lt. Dennis Appleton had predicted that he would have the medical examiner's report stating the cause of Bondeson's death by 2 P.M. Monday. Late Monday afternoon, Appleton stood before the waiting crowd of journalists on the Caribou courthouse lawn and made an announcement: The medical examiner had completed Daniel Bondeson's autopsy, but the results were being withheld.

There was a collective gasp from the reporters.

"Why the delay, Lieutenant?"

"They're examining items such as the weapon and some clothing," Appleton said.

"Is there suspicion that Daniel Bondeson was murdered?"

"They are just using an abundance of caution," Appleton replied, "so they don't have to get their eraser out next week and change it."

"Lieutenant, have you learned anything more about a possible motive for the poisoning? Is the motive unique to this community?"

"No, I don't think the motive is unique to this community. Early on there was some tugging and pulling to get people to admit some issues. I think it was probably something that was grinding at some people for some time. There were factions within that church. All the votes in that church didn't go ten-to-nothing. They sometimes went six-to-four."

Such comments about church dynamics fueled the already widespread belief that Daniel Bondeson could not have been responsible for the poisoning, since he had no interest in church politics and never engaged in GA's disagreements or feuds. "He didn't have a dog in that fight," one investigator remarked. In fact, he rarely went to church after the death of his father in May 2001.

Doubts about Daniel's role in the poisoning also aroused suspicion about his death. If he hadn't harmed anyone, why would he kill himself? Marilyn Kerr, who had become friends with Daniel about six years earlier, pointed to the fact that he had just bought a truck.

"He always had an old shitbox of a car—in plain English," Marilyn said. "And then he finally gets a halfway decent pickup. That was unusual. That boy—he had the first dollar he ever made. I mean, when they tell you he was tight, that's true. Danny was very frugal. And then all of a sudden he has a new truck."

Danny had also been planning for retirement. "He'd say, 'I've got to take X number of teaching jobs or work this many more hours to draw my full state retirement,'" Marilyn said. "So why would he care about retirement if he was going to kill himself?"

On Tuesday, May 6, the Maine Medical Examiner's office announced that Daniel Bondeson had committed suicide. Among the media, the announcement also gave weight to the probability that Daniel was responsible for the poisoning and that the case was about to be closed. Some reporters felt a bit of a letdown. After more than a week of living in a real-life episode of *Murder, She Wrote*, it appeared the mystery might be solved and the party was about to end. Then the Maine State Police dropped a bombshell: Daniel Bondeson had left a note containing "important information" that investigators would pursue. The arsenic poisoning remained an open case.

Erica Grace was trying to figure it out. *The medical examiner said Danny committed suicide, but that certainly didn't mean he poisoned the church coffee*, she thought. Danny was the type of person who would take the heat for anybody—especially anybody in his family. Danny would even shoot himself and then leave a note saying he was responsible for the poisoning, in order to protect someone else. Erica was convinced he would do that for anyone in his family, because Danny was like that.

Even if Danny was only indirectly involved, Erica reasoned, he would take full responsibility for what had happened. In fact, he would blame himself even if someone had stolen the arsenic from his farm. "That's just the way he was," Erica later said. "If he knew it came from his barn, and he'd had ample opportunity to get rid of it so this could have never happened, he'd say, 'All right, I've got to take the blame for this, because it really is my fault.' I can just imagine Danny sitting there reasoning with himself and saying that."

Erica was not alone. Among those who had known him, it was as if Danny were incapable of evil. Exculpatory theories abounded: He had supplied the arsenic to someone else, not knowing what it was for. He was tricked into doing it. He was protecting someone else. He didn't know it was arsenic.

As Doug McIntire followed the story in the news, he was developing theories of his own. "Shirley and Janet— that was my creepiest theory—the two spinster sisters that lived together," he said. "They were like the adopted grand-mothers of my children whenever they came up to visit. And when my kids were there, they'd always come up with McDonald's gift certificates for me, or give me some cash, and they'd say, 'Go get the kids something to eat today.' They were wonderful. They gave me quite a bit of cash when I left to move down here. I got a better sendoff than Scottie did. They had a party for me. They gave me around two hundred and fifty dollars. That was from the ladies of the church, I believe."

Doug quickly dismissed his Shirley-and-Janet theory as far-fetched. He thought Danny was a more likely suspect. Psychologically, it made sense—the quiet loner who snapped for real or imaginary reasons. But Danny wasn't passionate about the church. He had no zeal, no *oomph.* Doug hardly ever saw him in the church, and when he did, Danny was in the back corner, waiting to leave. *What did he do*, Doug thought, *just wake up one morning and say, "I have no reason to do this, but I'm going to do it"?* No, it sounded like he was a pawn of somebody else, someone saying, "Okay, Danny, this is what we're going to do."

Doug thought many of the news reports about Danny were off base. Yes, he had graduated from college, but he wasn't that bright. He was one of those people Doug would see and think, *Oh no, here he comes; he's going to talk to me.* He would go on forever about the potato harvest, and then the blueberry harvest, and an hour later he was still going on about it. He was socially inept and very awkward.

Investigators had heard tales of Danny's social clumsi-ness. "We heard Danny and a friend went out one night to go dancing," one detective recalled with a belly laugh. "Danny met a girl he liked, and he says to her, 'You have such beautiful teeth.' She says, 'Thank you.' Then Danny goes, 'Are they real?'"

Jerry Nelson also remembers taking Danny to a dance. Usually the wallflower at social events, Danny drank an entire pitcher of beer and "danced with every girl in the house." Jerry chuckled. "I've never laughed so hard in my life. Danny really whooped it up—he had a good time."

In the days following the poisoning, detectives were hearing the same thing repeatedly: Danny had no grudges or enemies at the church, and therefore had no motive to harm the congregation. Ron Morrill, whose father, Reid, died from the poisoning, said, "Danny was a very, very good friend. When Dad came back from his bypass surgery in January, Danny came over and shoveled off the roof. Mom and I are praying for his soul because we know that whatever comes of this investigation, we know that Danny would never, never want to harm Dad."

Because nobody believed that anyone, let alone Danny, would want to harm Reid Morrill, Reid's death drove home the random, cold-blooded nature of the crime. At first, Appleton said, "There was an unwillingness to accept that this could happen," and church members were less than forthcoming.

Under pressure from police, they began wracking their brains for possible motives and suspects. "They began to say, 'Well I guess we'd just better bare our souls, and even if something seems trivial or stupid, we're gonna say it anyway,'" Appleton said. As the medical conditions of Herman Fisher and Fran and Dick Ruggles began to improve, detectives pumped them and their families for information. Gradually, more details about the cliques and alliances at the church emerged, and one name kept coming up.

"We heard 'Norma Bondeson,'" a detective said months later. "People said her attitude is 'this is my church. If anything goes on, I want to know about it; I'm going to make the decisions.' "

"Quite a few of us think they should look at her," a local business owner told a reporter just days after the poisoning. "Karla Fisher thinks Norma did it; there's bad blood between them. Think about it—Norma's retired military, lieutenant colonel. She doesn't hear the word 'no.' "

Tiny seeds of innuendo such as this were scattered around the community and planted in the minds of investigators. In the fertile garden of small-town gossip, they quickly took root and grew into a thicket of suspicion surrounding Norma Bondeson.

Put Out the Fire with a Shovel

Lloyd Deschaine was munching a glazed doughnut and reading his legal pad through half-rim wire glasses. He had a long list of things to go over, and he wasn't even awake yet. He took a gulp of lukewarm coffee from a mug that read, "I'd rather be fishing."

"Okay, you guys, let's get started," he said. "I don't have much time. I have three interviews this morning. Millett— let's talk about the note."

"Somebody didn't get his beauty sleep," Millett said, batting his eyes at Deschaine.

"Millett, I'm gonna tell you right now, I'm in no mood for your fuckin' hilarity this morning," Deschaine growled. "Now, let's hear about the goddamn note."

"I'm sorry, Lloyd," Millett said. "You actually look very pretty."

Deschaine took off his glasses and laid them on the table. "Millett, if you—"

"Okay, okay, relax," Millett said. "The note. Let's see. Okay. It was laying there in the kitchen, and it's wet, and it's got little streaks of blood on it. So it's laying there, and I pick it up. It says, 'I acted alone. I acted alone.' "

"More than once, right?" Deschaine said, scribbling on his pad.

"Twice. And it's underlined twice. Then it says, 'I just wanted to give some people a bellyache like they gave me; then the word 'coffee' in parentheses. He said he didn't know it was arsenic, just wanted to make them sick. Then it named a few guys on the council, Herman Fisher—he's the president—and a few others—the old guys. One name is scrawled along the side, like it's an afterthought, like, 'Oh yeah, and him too.' But Reid Morrill's name isn't there. Danny thought those guys were mocking him, playing tricks on him."

"Is that what old Lutherans do for fun?" Bechard asked. "Play tricks on each other?"

Millett reached for a jelly-filled. He took a big bite and spoke with his mouth full. "The note doesn't make any sense."

"Hackett," Deschaine said. "What did Carl say?"

"I've been talking to him a lot," Hackett said. "He can be very moody, very obstinate. Then other times he's a regular guy, and he's very believable, very friendly. So I asked him. I said, 'Norma talked about bad things at the church. Is Danny the kind of guy that went up there and poisoned those people because his sister was having a hard time at the church?' And Carl said, 'No way.' He and Norma both said that. At first, they said Danny couldn't have done this at all. This is before they knew about the note. Neither one of them knew about the note."

"Where was the note again?" Bechard asked.

"On the kitchen table," Millett answered, popping the last of the doughnut into his mouth. "Hackett, pass me a napkin, will ya? Anyway, the note was kind of toward the back of the table. I almost missed it myself, spotted it just as I was about to leave for the nursing home. Carl would've easily missed it because the table had so much crap on it."

"Right," said Hackett. "So I'm talking to Carl. And he keeps saying Danny didn't do it, absolutely, Danny didn't do it. He couldn't do it because he's so stupid, as if we're talking about heart transplant surgery. So he's putting out this idea to forget about Danny and move on to a new suspect, right? And I'm thinking, maybe we should show him the note. Let's see what his reaction is. So I get the note and let Carl read it. So Carl takes the note; he reads the first line—stops. And he's deep breathing, and he has to get down, it's like he's gonna pass out as he sees the first two lines: 'I acted alone. I acted alone.' And five minutes before, remember, he was saying how absolutely certain he was that Danny didn't have anything to do with this. Then he reads those two lines, and he looks at me and says, 'He acted alone.'"

"That's what he said?" Deschaine said with a frown.

"That is exactly what he said," Hackett replied, nodding.

"Not 'Oh, God, Danny did it,' or anything like that?" Deschaine asked. "Just that he acted alone?"

"Right." Hackett folded his arms and sat back. "So what does that tell us?"

"That maybe he didn't act alone, and Carl knows it," Deschaine said.

"That's what I think," Hackett said.

"There's something else," Millett said. "I talked to a neighbor of Danny's, name's Ken Urquhart. He said Danny stopped by his house the morning of the poisoning and dropped off a bag of potatoes."

"What time was that?" Deschaine asked.

"About ten forty-five," Millett said. "He could have gone in the back door of the church at nine-thirty, threw the stuff in the coffeepot, and gotten back home, easy, in time to start loading up the spuds."

"What did Danny say?" asked Deschaine.

"He said, 'You want some potatoes?'" answered Millett.

"Wise guy," said Deschaine. "Did Urquhart notice anything strange?"

"Nah, he said Danny was the same as always," Millett

replied, "friendly. Urquhart really liked the guy. He said he wouldn't hurt a fly. He showed me a cat Danny gave him. He said Danny had rescued it from a trash heap."

"Heartwarming," Deschaine said, then turned to Hackett. "Did you ask Carl about the note, the names, and playing tricks?"

"Yeah," Hackett replied. "I said, 'What's he talking about?' And Carl says, 'I don't know.' So I asked him, 'Sometimes, do they make fun of him and stuff?' He says, 'Sometimes.' And he brought up the story about the field that was on fire next to that barn behind the house, and Danny was there, and his mother said, 'Danny, get a shovel and let's go over and take dirt and throw it on the fire and keep it from getting closer.' Later on, a couple of those guys—the ones in the note—made fun of the old lady for thinking he was gonna put out a fire with a shovel. Danny didn't like that, the fact that they made fun of his mother. Carl said things like that happened sometimes."

"Uh-huh," Deschaine said. "That's a little weird."

"Ya think?" Hackett said. "And other people have told us that Carl would scream at Danny right in front of them, call him names, and ridicule him in front of anybody because he was so stupid. Carl didn't tell me that, but I can see why he wouldn't. He probably felt bad that he used to yell at him. And what's ironic, the one guy that Danny liked the most, Reid Morrill, died. Talk about shitty luck."

"Well, he used arsenic for Chrissake, what did he think was gonna happen?" Deschaine said. "I mean, why not melt Ex-Lax on their hot fudge sundaes if he wants to give them a bellyache? Either he's even stupider than his brother thinks, or he wanted to kill them, or he didn't do it. Take your pick."

"Right," Hackett said. "None of the above makes sense."

"Hey, Hackett," Millett said. "I gotta know—how's the horny reporter? You serviced her orifice yet?"

"I thought you'd never ask," Hackett said with a grin. "Listen to this. I see her at the Chinese restaurant in Caribou, you know, the one with the buffet that got us all sick last year? And she's paying the check; she's with some guy, I think he's a photographer or something. So I pull her aside, and I look around, and I whisper, 'I'm about to give you the mother lode.' And her eyes get wide, and she says, 'Really?' I say, 'Your paper is gonna love you. But you gotta do a little work.' And she says, 'What?' I say, 'Well, if you go on the Internet and do a search, you'll find the story of a little Lutheran church in Sweden, back in the year 1606, the whole congregation got poisoned.' Then I say, 'I'm not sure—I think it was 1606; it might've been 1706.' Her eyes are like saucers. 'Really?' she says. I say, 'Find that—read it carefully, and a lot of the clues are right there. If you can't find it, I'll get it for you.' So then I give her my pager number, and I say, 'Where are you staying?' She goes, 'Caribou Inn.' I say, 'Okay, page me if you can't find it.' Then I get stern—all serious. And I look around, look at her, and I whisper, 'Keep this under your hat.' She's thrilled. She loves me."

"She's desperate," Millett said. "That's another quality I like in a woman. What's that Internet story you're talking about?"

"Who the fuck knows?" Hackett shrugged. "I made it up. Hey—there goes my pager."

"Okay, let's wrap this up, you clowns," Deschaine said, standing up. "I've got real work to do."

Holy War

In the days and weeks after the poisoning, Lt. Dennis Appleton repeatedly told reporters that the poisoning had stemmed from "church dynamics," including conflict over a communion table. The communion table, he said, was "one of the straws that broke the camel's back."

Doug McIntire was on the church council in 2002 when the table trouble erupted.

"I had the sorry duty of announcing the discussion," he recalled. "You could cut the tension with a knife. Barb Bondeson was fuming; I remember her saying, 'If I had known we were doing this today, my husband would have been here.' Her husband Paul set foot in the church maybe three times when I was there. Barb is always very easygoing, or so it would seem, but she seemed really upset about this."

Detectives mistakenly believed that the debate over the communion table divided the "traditionalists" from the "modernists" in the GA congregation. They thought the debate was of a spiritual nature. It is true that the use of a communion table would be a departure from tradition; it meant the minister would face the congregation, rather than the altar, while preparing communion. The rift, how-ever, had nothing to do with tradition. It was much more personal than that.

Since the dawn of Christianity, priests and ministers had celebrated the liturgy facing east, as did worshipers. But in the late 1960s the Second Vatican Council, or Vatican II, allowed Roman Catholic parishes more flexibility in deciding how to celebrate Mass, and priests began to face the congregation. Little by little, Lutherans followed suit, and today almost all seminarians are trained that way. "I believe that is more biblical anyway," Doug said. "At the Last Supper, Jesus was at the table with his disciples."

It remains, however, a matter of serious theological debate. "This world is not our heavenly homeland," argued Catholic theologian Rev. Joseph Fessio in his 1999 polemic *The Mass of Vatican II.* "We don't sit around in a circle and look at each other. We want to look with each other and with the priest towards the rising sun, the rays of grace, where the Son will come again in glory on the clouds."

Pastor Jim Morgan, who served as part-time interim pastor at GA, said that congregation by congregation, Lutheran churches were doing things the new way, "But the altar at GA remained as it was."

Gustaf Adolph, built in 1871, is on the National Register of Historic Places; remodeling the altar would deface a cultural treasure and compromise its historical integrity. Many church members were opposed to this, so it was agreed that any new altar would be portable, and the old one would remain as it was.

When the congregation first voted on the issue, there were three choices: a freestanding communion table, a portable altar that matched the existing one, or no change at all. "There were zero votes for no change," Morgan said. "They felt it was inevitable."

The arguments started when it came time to choose between the matching portable altar and the plain communion table.

"There were a couple of presentations," Herman Fisher

explained. "Ralph Ostlund volunteered to build something that would look exactly like the existing altar, but would be portable, to take in and take out. It would blend right in; it would match. Ralph offered to do that in memory of his wife, Edith. Now, who in their right mind is going to refuse Ralph? Such a wonderful gift, and Edith was so well loved in this congregation."

According to Beth Salisbury, Dick Ruggles was going to build the new altar on Ralph's behalf.

"Ralph was going to donate the lumber, everything," Beth said. "It would have been a movable altar that would have matched the rest of the woodworking and wheeled in and out. If you look upstairs in the church, there is a table and cabinet Dick made, and it matches everything else. The man is extremely talented."

The Bondesons, however, wanted to donate the other option—the plain, freestanding table, to be partially covered with a plain white cloth. This was to be in memory of several of their own deceased family members, including Barbara and Paul's son, who had been killed in an accident a few years earlier.

"Everyone was fighting about how it was going to look, who was going to do it, what would go on it," Beth said. "It was just a mess from day one. They fought about it everywhere and anywhere that anyone brought it up."

The final vote came up at a special congregational meeting in late 2002. According to Beth, only four families—the Bondesons, Ericksons, Andersons, and Landeens—wanted the plain table. "And when the vote came up," Beth said, "they brought people in that had not been to church for years. They brought a woman from a nursing home who had not been there in years—dragged her in from the nursing home!"

When the results were counted, the plain table won by a comfortable margin.

"So, how do you think that made Ralph feel?" Herman said. "The Bondesons said they'd give the table in memory of their parents, but offered Ralph the option of supplying the table. Ralph said 'Nope,' and who can blame him? So, the Bondesons gave the table."

"Because he was aware of how much the Bondesons wanted to do this, he stepped aside," said Pastor Morgan. "Ralph was responding to the emotional needs of the Bondeson family."

Barbara Bondeson got other family members to chip in and then mail-ordered the polished oak table. It was delivered to the Bondeson farm in Woodland, where it was stored in a barn until her husband, Paul, picked it up.

"I brought it home," Paul said, "and I put the legs together, and that same day I took it up to the church, and I lugged it in, and I set it in front of the altar."

The church council proceeded to ignore it.

"It was just brought in and put up by the altar, just set there," Herman said. "Nobody said, 'Okay, we brought the table in,' or anything. They dropped it off and placed it there. And then it got moved and set aside."

"When they actually brought the table out, I asked for a deck of cards," Beth said. "It was very, very tacky. It just sat there because it wasn't being used."

"I could see Herman snubbing the table because he couldn't get his way," Doug observed, "feeling that their power base had somehow been usurped by the Bondesons' group voting them down, and voting in what they wanted instead. It definitely would be a big defeat. You have to look at it as a political organization, not a church."

The church never used the Bondesons' communion table until the reclamation service—one week after the poisoning, two days after Daniel's death.

"The Bondesons ended up getting slighted," Doug observed. "They won the vote, but they didn't win in the end."

What Winter Would Bring

Paul Bondeson, Sr., was among the many folks in Aroostook County who cobbled together a livelihood working two or more jobs. He worked for many years as a mason, building sturdy hearths and a reputation for honesty. When he put up a chimney for Walden Babbidge in Limestone, Babbidge said, "He was the only fellow who charged me exactly what he said he would and not a penny more." In addition to bricklaying, Paul did maintenance work at Limestone Air Force Base until the early 1990s, when the base was shut down. He was, however, offered the chance to enroll in a job retraining program. Anticipating a casino boom on northern Maine's Indian reservations, he went to Las Vegas and took a course in slot-machine repair. Casinos, however, have not gotten past Maine voters, so Paul's newly acquired skill became a hobby, and he has several antique one-armed bandits in his house.

"I knew Paul because he was a carpenter," Doug McIntire said, "and I worked at the S. W. Collins lumber company, and I'd run into him a lot there. Nice guy, temperamental. Not like he would snap and scream at you or anything, but when he was mad, you knew he was in a bad mood. He's very direct. He won't hold back."

Paul was one of the few people in New Sweden willing to speak to reporters. He told anyone who asked that he did not believe his younger brother was involved in the poisoning, because he had never cared about the goings-on at the church. "Danny didn't give a shit about that stuff," Paul said. "His attitude was whatever happened, happened, and it was okay with him."

Paul, like his brother, had little interest in church politics and seldom, if ever, attended the Sunday service. But his wife, Barbara, was very active at GA, as was his sister, Norma. And Paul was aware of the splits and divisions. "There are about five people on that council," he told a reporter, "who are just a pain in the ass." He refused, however, to say who they were.

Paul told the *Boston Globe* that Danny was easygoing. "You could be digging potatoes and find a really rotten one, throw it to him, and it would splatter all over him, and he wouldn't react with anger."

That recollection did not surprise Marilyn Kerr. She had become acquainted with the Bondesons about seven years earlier at the American Legion in Stockholm, where Barbara served as president of the Ladies Auxiliary. "I had all the time in the world to do pretty much anything I wanted," Marilyn recalled, "so I was able to run errands with Barbara, or go with her to visit her mother."

Marilyn was appalled at how little respect Danny received from his family. "They treated Danny horribly," she said. "They made fun of him, laughed at him. They treated him just like the people of the town did, like an oddball. He was the whipping boy for the family. They would include other people in things they were doing, and he was an afterthought. He was Danny-go-get-wood, Danny-fetch-some-water, Danny-do-this. One day Barbara said, 'You're going to come over, and you're going to run errands with Marilyn.' She didn't ask him; she told him. And he did. He came over, got in the car, and rode to town."

In late 1996, Barbara and Paul Bondeson made their annual trip to Florida, where they stayed until spring. Marilyn kept an eye on their purple-shingled Cape Cod–style home while they were gone and promised to let them know about any problems. "It seemed like a good idea at the time," Marilyn recalled, "but then again, I had no idea what the winter would bring."

During this time Marilyn also got to know Danny Bondeson. "He said he needed a friend, and we could be friends," Marilyn recalled. "If he was going to be your friend, he was going to tell you that. If he didn't tell you that, you weren't going to be his friend. He was not all they made him out to be in the papers, not as weird as they made him seem.

"He wasn't much to talk. He was a nervous person; we could be riding down the road not saying anything, and right out of the blue he'd say, 'Nice day, huh?' It wasn't that he was odd, he was very shy. He was very smart. He went through college; he was a substitute teacher and worked as a nursing assistant. He wasn't stupid; he was just quiet.

"He used to go rake blueberries every year. He worked for the same person every year in the Blue Hill area. He saw the man's daughter, and she said he was too tight. He told me she said he was too tight. He said they either split or she paid. But he wasn't ashamed of the fact that he was frugal. And if you were with him, you paid your share.

"He used to come into the Four Corner Cafe, where I used to wait tables. It's up there where Northstar Variety is; the building's now gone. And they had a ninety-nine-cent breakfast special. And he'd get two eggs and a cup of coffee, which made it a dollar five, and he'd get his little plastic pouch out of his pocket—one of those little things that squeeze open—and he'd give me a dollar and a quarter and tell me to keep the change.

"Daniel was the nicest one of the bunch; he really was. He wasn't rude; he wasn't ignorant; he never said anything out of place. He was shy. He stayed home with his parents and made sure they were taken care of. He'd go to church if there was a social or something. He'd take his mother to services, and then when she died, if Harold wanted to go, he took Harold. But he didn't go regularly."

In mid-January 1997, Barbara returned to Maine for a two-week stay in order to tend to some business for the Ladies Auxiliary. Since her own home was occupied by Marilyn, she stayed with her daughter, Wanda, and her fiancé, Glenn Conroy.

On Saturday, February 1, toward the end of her visit, Barbara's thirty-year-old son, Paul Jr., drove up from his apartment in Beverly, Massachusetts, with his dog. He planned to do some snowmobiling. "He didn't tell anyone but just showed up," Marilyn recalled. "Barbara told him she didn't know where he'd sleep, since Wanda didn't have room for all of them."

Glenn and Wanda did, however, agree to take care of Paul's dog, and Glenn allowed Paul to borrow his snowmobile, a 1991 Arctic Cat Wildcat 700.

On Tuesday morning, Marilyn drove Barbara to the airport for her flight back to Jacksonville, and the following evening, Barbara called. Paul Jr. had disappeared. "She wanted to know if I could go to Wanda's and be with her while the guys searched for Paul."

Paul Jr. had been out of sight for a couple of days, but because he had no place to stay, no one had noticed. Finally, at 7:45 Wednesday night, Glenn and Wanda called the local game warden. They reported that Paul had not been seen or heard from since late Monday night, when he'd had too much to drink and had argued with a group of friends. Paul had left Jeff Page's house in a huff, Conroy said, and nobody had seen him since. Paul had left behind his eyeglasses, which he almost always wore. Conroy described what Paul was wearing: a red Yamaha jacket, an Arctic Cat helmet, black ski pants, and orange boots.

Paul was an experienced snowmobiler; in fact, he'd spent the entire day Monday sledding with a group of friends—Gardner Hersey, Brendan Fallon, Jon Sund, and Jeff Page. Nevertheless, Glenn said, Paul wasn't too famil-

All of the arsenic poisoning survivors, except Erich Margeson and Lois Anderson, are pictured in this photo.

FIRST ROW, LEFT TO RIGHT: Dick Ruggles, Fran Ruggles, Ralph Ostlund (with cane), June Greenier; SECOND ROW: Lester Beaupre, Shirley Erickson, Patsy Becthel, Dick Becthel, Reg Greenier, Peggy Bengtson; BACK ROW: Dale Anderson, Bob Bengtson, Herman Fisher.

Photo credit: Russell Kaye

Gustaf Adolph Evangelical Lutheran Church became a crime scene
in April 2003.

Photo credit: Christine Ellen Young

The kitchen at Gustaf Adolph Evangelical Lutheran Church.

Dr. Dora Mills, director of Maine Bureau of Health. After 9/11, Dr. Mills insisted that Maine obtain a stockpile of antidotes. If not for her foresight, the poisoning at GA would have become a multiple homicide.

Photo credit: John Pertel

Lieutenant Dennis Appleton gave daily news briefings at noon in the days following the poisoning, which made headlines around the world.

Photo credit: © 2003 *Bangor Daily News*, used with permission

Deputy Attorney General William Stokes.

Photo credit: Christine Ellen Young

The communion table donated by the Bondeson family was used by the church for the first time during the "reclamation service" one week after the poisoning, shown here.

Photo credit: © 2003 *Bangor Daily News*, used with permission

Ellie and Reid Morrill.

Photo credit: Courtesy Ron Morrill

Reid was known as a good-natured prankster.

Photo credit: Courtesy Ron Morrill

Reid was devoted to his family and drew great pleasure from
his grandchildren.

Photo credit: Courtesy Ron Morrill

Erica Grace Anderson spoke
with reporters outside the church
one week after the poisoning.

Photo credit: John Pertel

While GA had no pastor, Herman Fisher was president of the church
council and often served as lay minister and liturgist.

Photo credit: Ian Aldrich/Yankee Publishing Inc.

Lester Beaupre was in critical condition for several weeks
after the poisoning.

Photo credit: Ian Aldrich/Yankee Publishing Inc.

Lois Anderson with daughter Erica at Stan's.

Photo credit: © 2004 *Bangor Daily News*, used with permission

At 81, Ralph Ostlund skied 150 miles less than a year after hovering near death from acute arsenic poisoning.

Photo credit: Courtesy Ralph Ostlund

Detectives search near the chicken coop
where Daniel Bondeson was shot.

The Bondeson farmhouse.

Photo credit: Christine Ellen Young

The Bondesons put up No Trespassing signs
to keep out the media.

Photo credit: Christine Ellen Young

Ralph Ostlund in a traditional Swedish Laplander hat.

Photo credit: Christine Ellen Young

Daniel Bondeson (left) and Ralph Ostlund after a marathon.

Photo credit:
Courtesy Ralph Ostlund

iar with the trails in that area. Glenn and Wanda were getting worried. They'd already checked with several local motels, bars, and friends he might have stayed with. No luck. And perhaps most alarming, Paul had not even called to check on his dog.

On Monday evening, after finishing up on the trails, Paul and his friends had gone to Rainbow Cove Restaurant on Little Madawaska Lake. They had supper and a few drinks, and Paul had a few too many. "Paul was acting stupid," Jeff Page later reported to the game warden. "After we had eaten, we started to settle the tab; Paul wouldn't pay for his, so we all got kind of mad at him." According to Gardner Hersey, Paul refused to pay the bill, took off his boots, set them on the bar, and propped his feet up next to them. Paul was obnoxious, Hersey said, and began giving Pauline Lamb, one of the restaurant's owners, a hard time. The group decided to leave the restaurant and go to Jeff Page's house—without Paul. "Before we left I told Paul to go home or wherever and leave us alone," Page said. "I didn't want to have him over to my house, and the way he was acting, I didn't want him sledding with us the next day."

The friends arrived at Page's house at about 9 P.M. An hour or so later, Paul showed up. "I told him I didn't want him around and that he wasn't welcome here," Page said. "He took a beer out of the fridge. I told him again I didn't like how he had been acting that night; then Brendan and Gardy started getting on his case. This went on for maybe an hour. I kept offering to take him home myself, wherever he wanted to go, but he could not stay here." Page even offered to transport Paul's snowmobile in his pickup truck, but Paul refused. "I made coffee and took his beer away and tried to talk some sense into him, but he just wouldn't listen," Page said. Finally, when Page went outside and started to warm up his truck, Paul told the group he was "all set." Then he jumped on the Arctic Cat and took off.

After the Conroys' call to the wardens' service, Sgt. Fred Jackson drove out to Little Madawaska Lake to search for Paul. Several hours later, at about half past ten, he received a call from Erich Margeson, who said he'd noticed something odd that morning while driving his bus route— a track going into the trees off Lebanon Road. Margeson hadn't thought much of it until he got home and heard a message from Wanda saying her brother was missing on Glenn's sled. Margeson remembered the track he'd seen. He drove over to Lebanon Road, parked his truck, and peered over the snowbank. Only partially visible between the trees, there it was—a wrecked snowmobile. Margeson recognized it as Glenn Conroy's, and there were no footprints indicating anyone had walked away.

At about 11 P.M. Jackson met Margeson on Lebanon Road, and they hiked through the trees to the mangled sled, partially covered with fresh snow. Jackson took pictures; then, in the darkness, began probing the snow by the sled with his hands. Within minutes, he felt a body. He brushed away the snow. Erich watched as the flashlight's ray caught the shine of a helmet and then beamed on the face inside. It was his old friend, Paul Bondeson, Jr.

Marilyn had been fond of Paul. "He was smart," she recalls, "and when he was sober, he was very likable and fun." She says he drank too much, but "wasn't a mean drunk."

"Paul Jr. was a very well-loved character," said Pastor Jim Morgan of Trinity Lutheran Church in Stockholm. "He was kind of the golden child to a large segment of the community. He had that charisma that people liked."

Paul Jr. had also inherited his father's talent for masonry. He was an expert bricklayer; Paul Sr. had taught him the trade and then sent him off to school to refine his skills. "If young Paul could have just gotten off the bottle, he could have been the best mason in the area," remarked Dave Anderson.

Father and son, both of whom were born on September 11, had a stormy relationship, but when young Paul died, Marilyn said, "Their rocky years had healed, and they had made peace, the two of them." In fact, before leaving for Florida that winter, Paul Sr. had traveled to Massachusetts to visit his son.

In the years since, Paul Bondeson has spent his days in the company of loved ones—two brothers, both parents, and his only son—tending to their graves. He might be found leaning on his shovel, smoking a cigarette and offering plain wisdom: "When you're dead, you're dead. Until then, the sun's gonna come up in the morning, and it's gonna go back down at night." Then he'll look you in the eye, grin, and shrug.

On Friday, February 7, two days after young Paul's body was found, a story about his death appeared in the *Bangor Daily News*. "Alcohol and excessive speed were considered primary factors in the crash," the article said, and it quoted an unnamed friend who called him "intoxicated and obnoxious."

Barbara was devastated. Drunk and obnoxious—the article implied he deserved to die. It was a cold, callous eulogy for her sweet, funny young Paul. It was a swift condemnation, wrapped in a rubber band, tossed on the doorstep with last night's hockey scores, then thrown in the trash and forgotten. "Intoxicated and obnoxious"—the words were carved into Barbara's heart like a cruel epitaph. Her only son deserved better.

A Tempest in a Furnace

The communion table was not the only hot button at Gustaf Adolph; there was also the furnace. When the issue was raised in 2002, the congregation split into two factions, just as it had done over the communion table. "One side wanted to go with a new furnace and a whole new heating system," explained Herman Fisher. The other option was "to keep what we had and just update it, because it was supposedly a perfectly good furnace, and spare parts were still available."

"Dick Ruggles was the head of the property committee," Beth Salisbury recalled, "and he went to Dead River, Irving, and Ferris. Ferris gave the best estimate on the furnace, but the Andersons wanted Irving to have it.

"Ferris had the best deal. It included both the parsonage and the church. Dead River and Irving's estimates were just for the church, and their prices were more than Ferris.

"Dick's son Joe wound up working for Ferris, but this was after Dick got the estimate, so Dick told everybody. Then all of a sudden there was talk because his son works for Ferris, so he resigned off the property committee. He was going to resign off the council, and I told Fran, 'Don't you dare let him do that; that's not right because then they're gonna win. They'll have the vote and say on everything; they're gonna win. Don't let him do it. Tell him I'll be pissed off if he does.'

"Dick stayed on the council. Carl Anderson took over as president of the property committee. And we all voted on three estimates; we wanted three estimates. Carl only got one estimate. And I finally said, 'Listen, we all voted on three estimates; we only have one. I don't think we should present this to the church until we have three estimates.' And Herman agreed with me. We did say three. And I said, 'Look at the estimates we got, what's wrong with Ferris?' And all of a sudden, Dead River and Irving are saying, 'We didn't say it was that much,' and I'm thinking, this is just such bullshit.

"At the congregational meeting, there was so much yelling and screaming at the end that they just left it. This was January before the poisoning. Norma was there. Danny, I think he was there too. Usually they'd always get their families together whenever it came time for a vote so they'd have control of the vote. It really was bad. Even with the women's meetings—the Bondesons, Ericksons, Andersons, and Landeens—they'd all have a phone conversation beforehand and decide everything that the women's group was supposed to decide together. They would decide among themselves, so no one else would have a say because they were a majority at the meeting."

"We finally did decide to go with the Dead River plan," Herman said. "And the first thing we had to do was replace the one in the parsonage. The decision was made to go ahead with the new furnace in the parsonage and just update the one in the church, and we'd do that as we got the money. When we got the money, we went ahead and did the parsonage."

A Cooperative Witness

Erica was irate. The cops had left another message on the answering machine, which was all fine and dandy, but it was for Alicia—again. Detectives had interviewed Erica's mother and father twice, and her sister Alicia three times. Three! Here it was, almost two weeks after the poisoning, and they had not talked to Erica, not even once. Not only that—and this was what irritated her most—her name had come out. Oh, yes, it had. One of the detectives had asked Karla Fisher where Norma Bondeson lived in Massachusetts. "I can't think of the town she lives in," Karla had said, "but Erica Grace can tell you because Erica Grace has a friend who has a friend in that same town." *Okay*, Erica had thought, *they're going to be calling me any day now.* So she waited. And they didn't call. Here they were, talking to this one and talking to that one, and of course Erica knew exactly who they were talking to, because she knew every single person who lived in the town. She was probably closer to more people than Alicia ever was, and they had not even acknowledged Erica. Well, she would just have to march right up to town hall and introduce herself.

Erica drove over to the New Sweden Town Office and parked her car out back. She trudged across the parking lot, opened the ground-level back door, and went inside. "I'd like to speak to the detective in charge," she announced.

A short, chunky detective was sitting at a big table near the window. "That would be me," he said, popping a handful of peanuts into his mouth. He wiped his hands on his trousers and sat up. "Name, please?" he asked her.

"Erica Grace Anderson," she replied, arms folded and eyebrows raised.

The cop ran his pen down the sheet of paper in front of him. "Anderson, let's see . . . we have Lois, we have Alicia, we have Carl . . . " He looked back up at Erica. "We don't have you listed."

"Oh, you don't have me listed," Erica rolled her eyes. "All right, I'll go home." She turned as if to leave.

"Wait," the detective said. "You go to Gustaf Adolph?"

"Uh, yeah," Erica said over her shoulder, "and you've talked to everybody in my family at least twice. But if you're not interested—" She continued toward the door.

"Whoa," the cop said. Erica stopped. She waited a moment before turning around. "Here," he said, holding out a pen and a paper. "If you will just go right up those stairs, you'll find three detectives happy to help you." The detective grinned. "And if you would fill this out, we would be much obliged, Erica Grace."

"Okay," Erica said, blushing. He was kind of cute; not that she cared a whit. She took the pen and paper. *Creak, creak, creak*—Erica plodded up the noisy old stairs to the main floor.

Three detectives were in the front room, speaking in low voices and laughing. They stopped when Erica entered. One of the detectives approached her. He was tall and thin and wore glasses, the type who loved high-school chemistry and belonged to the Math Club. "Hello, young lady," he said. "I'm Detective Frank Bechard; this is Detective Jim Hackett, and this is Detective Mark Millett. Why don't you sit down right here?" He pulled out a chair next to a small table. "And you are?"

"Erica Grace Anderson," she replied primly, and took the seat.

Erica looked at the questions. Where had she been in the days immediately before the poisoning? Try to be as specific as possible.

She decided to start with Friday, Eureka night, and began writing: *At about seven o'clock, I went to Eureka and met Sam Carter before he went up country. Then I had to go get my cousin Ricky Scott, talked with him, then we left and got to Eureka about nine. It was Steven Anderson, Lisa Murray, Sven Bondeson, Ricky Scott, Jimmy Anderson, and Wayne Violet. We were drinking, playing the jukebox, and picking on each other.*

Erica stopped writing and looked up. "Detective Bechard?"

"Yes?" he said.

"Do you need to know how many drinks I had and who bought them for me?"

He looked at her for a moment. "No," he said, "we don't need to know that."

Erica shrugged. "It says to be as specific as possible." She went back to her writing. After a few minutes, she looked over again. "Detective?" she said.

"Yes?"

"I'm afraid one of my answers might give you the wrong idea about me."

"What do you mean?" he asked.

"Well, this thing asks where I was Sunday morning," Erica said. "I was home alone with my sister's boyfriend! We're just buddies, but it sure doesn't look too good on paper!"

Erica howled later on. "You should have heard the laughs I got when I said that. And they picked on me so bad. They were jovial. They made it so much easier."

She continued the questionnaire. Did you poison the coffee? *As if the person who did it is going to say yes*, Erica thought, writing *NO*. Why should police believe you? Because my mom and my very favorite uncle who I just love to death got poisoned, that's why. She shifted in the seat. Hmmph.

After she finished the questionnaire, Erica went back downstairs and handed it to the chubby detective. "I wrote a book," she said.

"Would you mind letting us take a blood sample so we can get some DNA?" he asked her.

"Nope, go ahead," she told him, and he pointed across the room to a laboratory technician. When she was finished with that, Erica sat down and waited for her interview.

"That's it," the detective said. "Thanks for stopping by."

Erica's heart sank like a stone. "No questions?" she asked.

"We know how to reach you," the cop replied. "We'll be in touch."

Guess Who's Here

In mid-May, Herman Fisher's dialysis catheters were removed, and a couple of days later he was released from Eastern Maine Medical Center. After weeks of hospital meals, he was eager to chow down on real food, so on the way home, he and Karla stopped in Houlton for some breakfast at a bustling diner with home-style cooking. Since it was not far from the state police barracks on Route 1, they decided afterward to run over and pick up Herman's clothes, which had been taken into evidence after the poisoning.

The Fishers walked through the big glass doors, and Herman approached the reception window, where he could see down the hallway. He stopped short at what he saw. Walking side by side with a detective, there she was.

"Karla!" Herman said. "Guess who's here."

Before Karla could respond, Norma Bondeson came out the door. At first Norma was startled; then she approached Herman and put her arm around him.

"How are you doing?" she asked.

"I'm fine," Herman told her.

"So you're out of the hospital for good?" Norma said.

"I sure hope so," Herman replied.

Norma approached Karla and reached out to touch her shoulder. "And how are you, Karla?" she asked.

Karla backed away. "Fine." *No thanks to you*, she thought.

"Well, take care," Norma said, and disappeared.

"Well, it's about time they got this bitch down here," Karla ranted. "Maybe the cops will be able to get some answers out of the big-shot lieutenant-colonel." She moved toward the window and looked outside.

"What are you doing?" Herman looked worriedly at his wife.

"I'm watching the car," Karla said, "because the woman's probably going to put a friggin' bomb in it."

Herman stared at Karla with alarm, then put his finger to his lips to quiet her down. Just then the door to the ladies' room opened, and out came Norma. She turned on her heels and exited through the front door.

"She must have heard everything," Herman said.

The Fishers chatted with the detective and retrieved Herman's clothes. When they went outside, Norma was sitting inside her small white Nissan sedan. Herman and Karla walked past her and got into their car, and as Herman turned onto Route 1, he peered in his rearview mirror.

"Karla! Norma's going back in the police station," he said. "She waited until we left and went back in."

Karla leaned back in her seat and smiled. "I'd love to be a fly on the wall for that interview." She sighed, then closed her eyes and relaxed for the hour-long ride to New Sweden.

As Herman settled in at home, Bill Stokes was preparing to try another homicide case in Aroostook County. The savage murder of a beautiful young woman, Tara Bell, had taken place the previous December in Limestone, about twenty minutes from New Sweden, allegedly at the hands of a jealous wife. Stokes scheduled some witness interviews and decided to drive the five hours north from Augusta on a Sunday afternoon.

His trip did not go as planned.

"I'll never forget the day," Stokes said. "It was my daughter's recital, you know, those dance recitals? Have you been to those? They go on interminably; your ass is sore and everything else. I've been through this now for twelve or thirteen years, whatever it is, since she was five. And now she's the star of the show.

"I had gotten a car; it was a Dodge Neon. It was like a Barney color; I called it the Barneymobile. I had packed everything up; I was going to go up Sunday afternoon. I was going to interview witnesses Monday and Tuesday and come home Tuesday afternoon.

"I figured I'd leave right after the recital; I figured the recital would be over by four. It went on till like, five-fifteen, five-thirty, and so now I'm getting nervous. And I'm actually thinking about this, because you know, my daughter's friend was killed. Mallary Dulac was killed in Sydney a year earlier hitting a moose; this was June 2002, two days after school was out. It was awful, the worst day of my life, the worst week of my life; it was terrible just dealing with, you know, kids, of course. It was just terrible.

"But in any event, I was actually thinking about it on the way up. I wanted to go when I had plenty of light. And I remember driving nonstop right through to Oakfield, where you head up to go to Route 11, or maybe it was the Smyrna exit. I pulled in and I got a carton of milk and a candy bar; I didn't want to stop and have supper. I was worried that I'd lose the light, and I kept heading up.

"A black cat ran out in front of me, and of course I'm saying that was weird; I'm thinking about that as I drove up. So I'm going like a sonofagun, and I was losing the light. And it got to be like nine o'clock; I was about a mile or two miles from Ashland, and a car came at me and blinked its lights, and I thought they were trying to tell me to dim my high beams.

"Next thing I knew, this thing was in front of me. And

the only words I remember thinking as it happened—I said, 'This is it.' And I turned my head to the right, and I slammed on the brakes and waited for the impact. Frankly, I expected a blow to the head. And it hit the windshield, and it bounced over the car, and then I looked out the window, and I saw the moose. He looked at me as if to say, 'What'd you do that for?'

"It shattered the glass; you know how that glass just pulverizes. I had a scratch on my hand. And the moose had to be put down; it was hurting. I was very fortunate because it was a young moose; they said it was like a year old. If that had been a full-grown moose, I would have had my head crushed.

"I'm not a moose fan. They're dangerous. We had five of them last week, car-moose collisions—in a day—all over the state, as far south as Falmouth. They're funny animals; I have no real use for them. And the problem is they have no known predators. Who the hell's bigger than they are in the Maine woods? Who's going to attack a moose? They have no predators, except us, and they don't think of us as predators, so they come out and wander on the road; they don't know shit from Shinola about getting on a road, and you can't see them.

"So there's the car, ruined. I get picked up by police; they sent up a car to get me, and I did my interviews. I was getting ready to try that case, the murder of Tara Bell, a beautiful girl. She was twenty-seven or twenty-eight, in the process of getting divorced from her husband, and she was running a day-care center. In the meantime, Laura Kirk and her husband are in the process of getting a divorce; Laura Kirk is clearly a very troubled woman. The husband, Gerald Kirk, had custody of the kids, and he used Tara Bell as day care.

"That summer, it was in 2001; Gerald and Tara developed a friendship. He would drop the kids off in the morning, and pick them up in the evening, and they would talk, and one thing led to another, and they became friends. He really treated her nicely, and she was beautiful. And while this was all going on, Laura was getting wind that they were becoming friends and getting closer, and she was getting increasingly jealous and making remarks about 'Gerald would take me back except for that Tara.'

"Things were going wrong with Laura. Everything was going wrong with her. And one night in December, she parked the van about four hundred feet down the road, on a potato road, and snuck up to the house, and came in and slashed Tara to death. Vicious. With a young baby in the house, killed her in her own kitchen—just a vicious killing. It was just a nasty, nasty killing.

"So I did my interviews, and that night there's big news on the TV. Police announce they have another suspect in the New Sweden arsenic poisoning. And I'm thinking, what's going on? What's that all about?"

Stokes was aware that since the beginning, Dennis Appleton had been saying investigators were trying to rule out the possibility of a conspiracy, but now his words were much more tantalizing. "I know Daniel Bondeson didn't act alone," Appleton told reporters. "We're strong on that position." Appleton also said he did not like to use the word "suspects," but detectives had whittled down the list of "persons to talk to" to six to ten church members. That short list included the Bondesons. "Some of them may be telling us the truth," Appleton said. "Some of them, in the end, may not."

Stokes was apoplectic. "I called his superiors, and I said, 'What the hell's going on? Why are you saying this? Will you please—why are they saying this stuff?' They said, 'Well, you know, we believe this . . . ' And I said, 'I don't care what you believe—who cares?' I made no secret of the fact that I think they said too much."

Dysfunction Junction

"All right, who's on first?" Deschaine was looking over his notes. "Bechard, you're it. Tell us all about Sister Norma."

"You know something?" Bechard said. "It's funny you say that, Deschaine. That's exactly what Norma reminds me of—a nun. Sister Mary Norma. Mother Superior."

"What did you find out?"

"We searched the house in Amesbury," Bechard said. "Found a couple of things that were interesting. She has a Merck manual—not unusual for a nurse. But it was open, and guess what she'd been boning up on—arsenic anti-dotes."

"Hmm," Deschaine chewed his pencil and stared off for a moment. "Not exactly a smoking gun. You could take it either way."

"Yeah, I know," Bechard said. "Also, we talked to her old boyfriend, Sandy Carlisle. He doesn't think she had anything to do with the poisoning."

"How well does he know her?" Deschaine asked.

"Very well," replied Bechard. "They've known each other about twenty years; lived together for ten. After they broke up, she stayed in the Amesbury house; he moved to New Hampshire. Now he's selling the Amesbury house; that's why she's moving back to the old Woodland farm. She was forced into retirement. So she's lost her career, and now she's losing her home.

"Now, get this: A reporter told me she tried to talk to Norma after church, after Sunday school was over. She went back into that social hall, and Norma was with Barbara Bondeson. They were leaning over the piano, whispering. The reporter walks up and says, 'Are you Norma Bondeson?' Norma and Barbara go wild; Norma charges after the reporter and says, 'No, I'm not!' Barbara yells, 'No reporters!' They all but shove the reporter out the door and slam it. A bit of an overreaction, wouldn't you say?"

"What do you make of it?" Deschaine asked.

"Norma is a woman who wants to be in control," Bechard said. "See, to break her, you've got to take her out of her environment. The reporter was challenging her in her own environment. That's good psychologically. She's got to feel her world is closing in on her psyche; her world is coming apart. The church is a focal point. I don't believe she is deeply religious. My theory on her is she's got a long-standing relationship with the church, but the church transforms into her. This is about her and her family; it's about control. It could be a Kiwanis hall; as long as she's in charge, it doesn't matter.

"So, it's all about control, and now she's losing control. When she came in for DNA, it was a fucking performance. It was raining, and everyone else jumps out of the car; they don't care where the puddles are. Norma gets out and pops open her umbrella like Mary Poppins to walk twenty feet— twenty stinkin' feet. It's a performance. Then she comes in, and it's another performance; she's a person who's got to be in control."

"What about Danny?" Hackett asked. "I mean, c'mon, he wasn't wrapped too tight—let's face it."

"Look," Bechard said, "this is Dysfunction Junction. The Bondesons are a bunch of screwballs. The straw that broke the camel's back was the communion table. It was brought to the church by Paul Sr. without approval. They didn't get the reaction they had hoped to get, didn't get the accolades they so justly deserved."

"There's a piece missing here," Deschaine said. "It's called motive. You said Norma and Barbara Bondeson were whispering. What's Barbara's story?"

"Okay, this is interesting," Bechard said. "Barbara is the one who bought the communion table. It was in memory of several of the Bondeson relatives, including Barbara's son. He was killed six years ago in a snowmobile accident. It was apparently kind of a scandal; he was drunk."

"Okay, now that's what I call motive," Deschaine said. "There's passion there—a bereaved mother, angry that her son's memorial is scorned by the church."

"True," said Bechard. "But Barbara passed her polygraph."

"I'm not surprised," Millett said. "I don't see Barbara as having that in her. But Norma—here we've got a hard lieutenant-colonel, street smart. She's patronizing as hell. As you start to ask a hard question, she'll throw out a sarcastic remark. She tries to twist it so she can find out what we know. She'll ask questions like, 'Who told you that?' If you ask her about a church matter, she'll say, 'This is very important. I want people to know where I stand on votes and on issues.' Like a congressman. I said, 'Tell me about the politics of the church,' and she says, 'I don't know much about the politics. And it has a name. It is Gustaf Adolph Lutheran Church.' She plays these little word games, you know?"

"Get this," Bechard said. "We're asking her where she was the weekend of the poisoning, right? And she says she was in Massachusetts, that she left Saturday after the bake sale. But someone said her car was parked outside the church late in the afternoon. They swear they saw it there. We ask Norma; we say, 'If you were on your way to Massachusetts, how could your car have been parked outside the church?' She says, 'A miracle.' She's a wiseass. Another thing she said: 'You don't have to be present to be an active part of an event.' What the hell does that mean? So we play a little hardball with her. We say, 'Okay, Norma, we know you know what happened. Why don't you just tell us?' She says, 'I'll take what I know to my grave.'"

Millett sat up and slammed his hand on the table. "I'm going to end this case right now," he said. "I'm going to go over and teach Fran Ruggles how to shoot, and I guarantee Norma will be gone."

There was a roar of laughter.

"A lot of the trouble over there does seem to begin with the ladies of the church," Deschaine said.

"I always say if it weren't for women and liquor we wouldn't have jobs," Hackett said.

"What about the twins?" Deschaine asked.

"Shirley and Janet?" Bechard said. "They're not really twins, just sisters."

"Yeah, I know, I know," Deschaine said. "But I can't tell them apart. What's the story with those two? Shirley went to the hospital, and they asked her there if she had coffee, and she said yes. She told them at first she didn't drink it. Then she said she did."

"Shirley had a sip," Bechard said. "She took a sip from somebody else's cup just to see what all the fuss was about."

"Okay," Deschaine said. "But I understand these two usually knock people down going for the coffeepot. And that day, they didn't drink it."

"They were going to a brunch later on," Bechard said. "I asked around about those two. I hear they're like Switzerland—they don't fight with anybody."

"I've asked Carl about Norma a few times," Hackett said. "I can ask that guy anything at all, and he isn't shaken by it. So I went in, and I said, 'Why do so many people think Norma did it?' And then I told him the whole theory about Norma wanting to be in control, about how she considers it her church, and so forth. And he says, 'Gee, I don't see it that way.' And I'll say, 'I think you know a lot more about what's gone on than what you're saying.' He says,

'Well, I can see why you think that.' I can be very blunt with him; I can say anything to him, and he takes it fine. I could tell him I think he's personally responsible, and I can see it now, he'll give me a little shrug, and he'll say, 'Probably other people are going to think that, too.' He just shrugs it off, and then he invites me up to meet his son.

"So I asked him, point-blank. I said, 'You seem to be very nonchalant about this death.' And he gave me the impression it was a family thing. He said they're close, but they're used to it; on a farm you get used to death. Animals die; people die. It's the natural order of life. People die."

"What about Norma's little darling, Finn?" Millett asked. "Maybe he did it for the family. He's just a kid. Maybe he thought he was saving his family from the big meanies at the church."

"That's really a stretch, Millett," Hackett said. "The kid had the flu, for crying out loud. There is no indication that he had anything to do with this. He'd been sick for almost a week."

"Why did Carl act so defensive?" Millett asked.

"Because he thought a boneheaded cop was accusing his ten-year-old of attempted mass murder," Deschaine said. "I can understand his irritation, Millett, and personally, I think your Finn theory should go the way of the grassy knoll."

"It's just a possibility, all right?" Millett said, "My money is still on Norma. Okay, maybe it wasn't the kid. But somehow, she came up with a way to do it and not be seen."

"What about the bake sale Saturday?" Deschaine asked. "She was there, right? Danny was there. Either of them could have gone into the kitchen and started messing with the coffeepot, and people would have thought they were just making coffee."

"Herman says he rinsed out the pot Sunday morning," Hackett said. "But maybe he didn't clean it out well enough to remove all the arsenic."

"Okay," Deschaine said, closing his notepad. "Let's keep going on this and meet tomorrow at nine."

"Wait!" Millett said. "We're forgetting the most important question."

"What's that?" Deschaine asked, looking puzzled.

"Has the horny reporter given it up yet, Hack?"

Deschaine rolled his eyes, stood up, and left the room. Bechard followed behind.

"If I tell you," Hackett said with a smirk, "it will lend a whole new meaning to the term 'internal affairs.'"

"Gimme five, brother." Millett grinned, throwing out his hand. "In love and war, persistence pays."

The Furry Hand

Lester Beaupre woke up in a place he didn't recognize, and he had no idea who he was. The room was semi-dark, a few streaks of afternoon sunlight filtering through the window blinds. He heard voices outside the open door. There was a TV on somewhere. His throat was killing him, and he was thirsty. The wall was covered with greeting cards—maybe a hundred or so. On the table by his bed were eyeglasses; he put them on and peered more closely at the cards. "Get Well Soon!" several of them read. "Thinking of you during this difficult time." His stomach tightened. *Who am I?* he wondered. *Why am I here?* He scanned the cards on the wall again and saw a handwritten name in big block letters. "Lester," the card read. "Sorry to hear you're under the weather."

"Oh, okay, I'm Lester." He lay back and closed his eyes just as a nurse walked into his room. She walked past his bed, glanced at his IV, went into the bathroom and turned on the light. She didn't close the door, and he could hear her rustling around, and then a steady trickle in the john. Lester stifled a laugh, scooted over to the side of his bed, and pushed the door shut with his foot. He heard a gasp, a moment of quiet, and then the *whoosh* of a flushing toilet. When the nurse came out she didn't even look embarrassed.

"You gave us quite a scare, Mr. Beaupre." She smiled. "It's nice to see that you're feeling better. Your wife and family are going to be happy to see you, too. They'll be back from lunch at any moment."

Lester recognized his wife when she walked in.

"What's happening?" he asked her.

"Remember at church?" Louise said.

"Yeah, that food poisoning?"

Louise pulled up a chair and sat down next to Lester's bed. "It really wasn't food poisoning," she told him. "It was arsenic poisoning."

"Arsenic? Who else is here?"

"Herman, Dick, Ralph . . . "

Lester interrupted her, "How's Ralph?"

"He's doing well." Louise hesitated for a moment, and then went on, "Danny did it."

"Danny? Really?"

"He committed suicide."

Lester was baffled. "When did he do that?"

"On your birthday."

Lester just sat eyeing Louise for a moment. "Got any good news?"

Louise laughed. The arsenic hadn't hurt her husband's sense of humor.

Lester looked around the room. He had seen a lot of strange things over the past few weeks. It had started with the furry hand. A game warden had been in his room doing paperwork on Lester's food tray, and he had left the paperwork there. A snake came in and hid under the paperwork. All of a sudden, Lester saw this big furry hand—it might have been a tarantula, but it looked more like a furry hand. The hand slid its hairy pointed fingers underneath the paperwork, grabbed the snake, and went off with it.

A rat had come into his room, too. It was the same rat he

remembered from Vietnam. Lester's unit had spent most of its time out in the bush, but once every two weeks, the soldiers would go back to home base to stock up on supplies. One night Lester was staying in someone else's bunker, and he had to sleep on the floor underneath a table. He had been asleep for a few hours when he woke up with a pain in his arm. Reaching over to see what it was, he felt whiskers and a scratchy foot. It was wriggling. He slapped it, and the rat bit down on him hard, not letting go. Lester screamed, jumped up, and hit the table, sending ashtrays, books, and a water glass flying. His bunk mates woke up to see Lester in a frenzy, hollering and beating on his arm until the rodent finally let go and scurried off.

Afterward, Lester was told he needed a series of fourteen rabies vaccinations, to be injected into his stomach lining. He endured one of the shots, then got on a helicopter and went back out to the bush.

That rat came to the hospital and terrorized me again, Lester thought. *But now I'm not sure what's real and what's fantasy. Is Louise really sitting here?*

"So where's everybody now?" Lester asked her.

"They're all up to the physical-therapy floor. You were in a drug-induced coma for two weeks, and they pulled you out of it, and your throat was so constricted that they had to put you back under and give you a tracheotomy."

Gradually, Lester started to adjust to his surroundings. Now that he was conscious, he had to begin physical therapy. He and Ralph were on the same schedule and had sessions together. "We used to play soccer," Lester recalled. "The nurses would hold us up and we'd kick the ball at each other."

Lester remembers one of the nurses as "kind of aggressive."

"She was holding Ralph, telling him, 'Kick it harder to him, Ralph!' and Ralph kind of looked at me," Lester said, "and she kept bugging him. So all of a sudden Ralph says, 'I don't want to do this anymore.' She turned around and was taking him toward his wheelchair, and I took the soccer ball and I kicked it, and hit her right in the butt."

Lester laughed at the memory, then continued. "She ended up being my therapist. One day I was working out on the machine. She said, 'How are you doing?' I said, 'Well, if you stop treating me like a little baby and put some extra weights on this, maybe I could get better.' And she looked at me, and she piled the weights on it. And I was able to lift them. She was really pushy. She was good."

Lester's biggest problem was walking. He was numb from the knees down, and his thighs hurt from the antidote injections. "That was very painful," he said. "I remember the first time I walked, this nurse was holding me. I was walking real slowly, and my knees gave out so fast that on the way down, she grabbed me. I didn't fall."

After a while, Lester would use a wheelchair as a walker. He walked as often as he could. "I did more than I was supposed to," he says. "I wanted out of the hospital. I told them I was going to leave the next Friday, and they laughed. But I did. I left that Friday."

Elvie Johnson's Murder

Reid Morrill's death was the first homicide in Maine's Swedish Colony since March 1988, when a ninety-year-old widow, Elvie Johnson, was murdered in her Stockholm house. Elvie was a "good old Swede," according to her granddaughter, Betty Jean Gallagher, and "a good, believing Christian who always wanted to look at the best of what people had to offer." So when Elvie hired two local teenage boys to help her with odd jobs around the house, her family wasn't surprised by her kindness, but they were worried about her safety. Robert Rossignol was known to drink and use drugs. He and his younger brother, Claude, worried Elvie's family, but because they were from a disadvantaged family, Elvie felt sorry for them and wanted to see that they had pocket money. Betty Jean and other family members often warned Elvie that she was too trusting of the boys, both of whom swaggered like street toughs.

"They weren't fine, outstanding characters, and you knew that they could be kind of slippery and slimy," Gallagher remembers. "We used to say, 'Nana, you should be a little bit more careful.' And she'd say, 'Oh, they're good boys; you have to see the good side of them. If you treat them right, they'll treat you right.' And we kept telling her, 'You know, they really can't be trusted.' But she'd say, 'I have no reason not to trust them.' Her attitude was you respect them because they are human. Maybe it's their upbringing, they don't have parental guidance, and someone just needed to show them kindness."

On Monday morning, March 14, 1988, Urban Acoin took his morning stroll to the Stockholm Post Office to pick up both his mail and Elvie's. It was something he did for his neighbor each day, and often the two of them would chat. Normally, Urban didn't knock on Elvie's door; he would just open it and walk in. But today the door was locked. Urban jiggled it a second time. Then he looked through the window and saw his friend lying on the sofa. He went home and contacted Elvie's grandson.

What Brent Johnson found inside his grandmother's house was so grotesque he has never discussed it. "Brent doesn't talk about it at all," says Betty Jean, his sister. "Even in family conversations he doesn't." Elvie had been attacked by a madman—raped, strangled, and stabbed with several knives.

Betty Jean was attending school in Portland when her parents called on Monday morning with the news that Nana had been murdered. She came home right away and was immediately questioned by police. "I had to sit down and be interrogated," she remembers, "and everyone who had breathed on the house got interrogated, and the police were all over."

Five days after Elvie's death, police arrested Robert Rossignol. He had given police a videotaped confession. "He said he didn't know why he did it, because she was the only one nice to him," Betty recalled. "That was hard to take."

Meticulous evidence collection yielded positive DNA samples and Rossignol's thumbprint on Elvie's thigh. Rossignol, who was seventeen at the time of the crime, was tried as an adult and found guilty of murder. He was sentenced to seventy-five years at the Maine State Prison in Thomaston. With good behavior, he could be out in fifty.

Fifteen years after her grandmother's murder, Betty Jean was struck by how differently the Maine State Police appeared to be handling the New Sweden arsenic poisoning.

"With the New Sweden case, they always met at the courthouse in Caribou," she said. "With my grandmother, the crime scene was set up across from her house at the fire department; they didn't meet in Caribou. They set up the crime scene where the action was, so they could see who was coming up and down the street. They didn't care about the reporters so much. They were on the scene."

Midsommarfest

The weather on June 21, 2003, was perfect for the first day of Midsommar. Yellow sunshine warmed the royal-blue sky, matching the colors of the Swedish flag. Purple and white lupines embroidered the landscape. At seventy-seven, Alwin Espling still got up early and tromped through the tall, dew-soaked field next to the New Sweden Post Office to clip flowers and branches. He would then carry them away in buckets to later adorn a thirty-foot-high *majastang*, or Maypole. Against a backdrop of fiddlers and wildflowers, white linen shirts, and whirling patchwork skirts, the festival bestowed magic upon the town like a long-awaited fairy godmother.

Nancy Jepson Troy, a native of New Sweden, returned each year from Ohio for a weekend of delightful nostalgia. She remembered digging potatoes on her parents' farm and working in the fields every autumn, when area schools would close for three weeks so that children could help with the harvest, earning money for school supplies and clothes. She remembered crisp, clean air and the cool aroma of fresh potatoes and rich earth. She loved it all, despite the backaches and sore knees that came from bending all day. Her husband had participated in the harvest one year, the last year her own father planted potatoes. She had told him it built character and he had agreed, but admitted it was the hardest work he'd ever done.

Nancy knew that this was a unique and special place, but that tragedies could happen anywhere. She also knew that New Sweden's heart had been broken.

Midsommar got into full swing at 5:30 Saturday morning with the annual *Fiskare Frukost*, or Fishermen's Breakfast. A few of the Lutheran men who usually prepared eggs, bacon, and potatoes for the occasion were still at home recovering from the arsenic poisoning. Lester Beaupre was just out of the hospital. Dale Anderson's legs were still bothering him, but he handed out tickets for the door prizes. Herman Fisher was flipping pancakes.

There were plenty of helpers, lots of food, and a line of hungry patrons snaking out of the small meetinghouse at Thomas Park. Church members ignored reporters, who dined with their notebooks in hand. Norma Bondeson, wearing shorts and knee socks, sat down at a table next to Pastor Jim Morgan. She conversed and laughed with acquaintances, and made an attempt at humor that may have been well meaning, but went over like a stink bomb.

"It was June twenty-first, my wedding anniversary," Lois said, "and Carl was working at the breakfast, and he sat down with me for a few minutes, and we joked because he was taking me out on our anniversary to a fisherman's breakfast. The girls were all around, and here comes Norma headed right for me, and she said she thought I looked so good! 'That poison must have done something for you,' she said, 'you look so much better.' I was flabbergasted. I didn't know what to do."

Norma took great pains to avoid the media. Rather than walk by two reporters chatting outside the breakfast hall, she asked a friend to get his pickup truck, back it up to the entrance, and drive her about fifty feet past them.

By the time breakfast was over and the frying pans

packed away, Midsommarfest had moved to the center of town, where art displays and music were featured and homemade ice cream was served by Ellie Morrill and several other women of the church. Reporters and photographers jockeyed for position to see the trimming of the Maypole outside the Capitol School and Museum, and floral wreaths were woven into young girls' hair. Townspeople were eager to show off their heritage and mark the occasion with pride, yet some were resentful of the media's presence, muttering insults to reporters.

Beads of sweat dotted the foreheads of women dressed in heavy Swedish costumes, and a near calamity with the Maypole underscored the tension in the air. Just as a group of men tried to lift the heavy structure into place before several hundred onlookers, the Maypole sagged and then toppled to the ground, nearly hitting Sven Bondeson, nephew of Danny and Norma. There was a collective gasp from spectators, and for a moment it appeared that the treasure of Midsommarfest was going to become a casualty. Then a second attempt to right the pole was successful, and Sven was clearly relieved.

An affable fellow in his mid-twenties, dark-haired and handsome with a distinctive, booming voice, Sven is the last full-blooded Swede in the Colony and one of the few members of the Bondeson family willing to talk to the media. He seemed to relish his role at Midsommar. Driving up in a Triumph convertible, he was regally dressed in pantaloons and a colorfully tasseled Laplander hat, acquired during a visit to Finland. His wife, Connie, looked stunning, wearing full Swedish garb and a crown of flowers in her long cornsilk hair. Sven and Connie made a beautiful pair, the king and queen of the festival—unless you ask Erica Grace, that is.

"Oh no, no, no, no—wrong!" Erica said. "She thinks she's all that and a box of Cracker Jacks. That's what I tell everybody. Sven didn't really talk to her most of the time because he went on the horse ride with me, and he came back, and was hanging out with me. They got in a fight up there. She went home because she was pissed he was talking to me and thought there was something going on between us. And it ended up he took her Jeep, and Sven and I ended up sitting next to Northstar Variety, drinking.

"He's just dumb. He divorced her; she took him for all this money. Then all of a sudden, 'Oh, but I love her,' and they hooked back up. Then they were having rocky times—nobody really supported him going back with her just because of the way she treated him last time—but we all stood by him and dealt with it. And that went on, and they broke up. And it's over; it's done, and he said he'd never go back to that."

Lester Beaupre had been out of the hospital for only a few weeks when he showed up at Midsommarfest. Watching the festival from under a big shady tree, he was bewildered by the behavior of his fellow church members.

"I find the way they're not dealing with this strange," he said. "They ask you how you are, but nobody from the church has actually talked to me about the homicide part of this ordeal. And these are the people that should be interested the most. Maybe it's one of them Swede things, I don't know. I'm French Acadian, and if this would have happened in my neighborhood—I mean the state troopers would be getting badgered every day."

Lester was also frustrated with the police. He felt they'd planted a land mine by publicly stating that the crime was a conspiracy and then not telling church members if they were in danger or what they were doing about it.

"I wish they'd say, 'We haven't forgotten about you guys. We're still working on the case,' you know? Some people are asking, 'What does it mean—that there is somebody among us who is capable of killing people?' And maybe it's somebody we talk to every day?"

With the nerve endings in his feet and calves still tingling, Lester felt strange and weak, unable to work more than just a few hours at his carpentry. He was afraid his legs would give out underneath him, and worried about what the future had in store.

Lester took a pass on one of the highlights of Midsom-marfest, the smorgasbord.

The word *smorgas* is the equivalent of "open sandwich," and *bord* is Swedish for table, but a smorgasbord is not a table of sandwiches. It is much more enticing: heaping platters of herring dishes, Swedish meatballs, salmon, sal-ads, bread, and potatoes served in almost every imaginable form. One of the sittings for the feast was at the Gustaf Adolph church. The idea that someone who helped poison the church coffee could be concocting a Midsommarfest treat was disturbing, but townspeople like Doug Anderson, president of the Maine Swedish Colony, gave little sway to the notion of a mass murderer in their midst.

"I feel that it was just an isolated incident," he said, "and from what I hear, if Danny did put it in the pot, he just wanted to give them a bellyache."

Doug, who was born in New Sweden, left as a young man and worked in sixteen different states. "I had been in the hubbub working in construction, electrical construc-tion, moving from one city to another; worked on the casi-nos in Atlantic City, car plants, and steel mills."

He is not a member of Erica's clan. "I'm not related to any of the other Andersons around here," he said. "There's five different groups, and everybody assumes since you're an Anderson, you're related. Well, we're not."

Doug and his wife had been living on the Wisconsin line between Chicago and Milwaukee when suburban sprawl nudged them back to New Sweden. "It's sort of laid-back, and that's what I was looking for," he said. "I just don't like being pushed and crowded and shoved and banged, stand-ing in lines. Stuff like that. This is a place I don't have to do any of that."

Now Doug's life was simple. He mowed the cemetery lawn, served as president of the Swedish Colony and trustee for the town museum, and was caretaker of Thomas Park. "And on top of that," he said, "I try to get my own place looking decent."

This year Doug didn't have as much assistance with the

Midsommarfest preparations as he had in the past because so many of his helpers had been poisoned. "Ninety-five percent of 'em that are sick are the worker bees that, like in any organization, they're the ones that done the work," he said. "This is all volunteer. I get no pay for this, and those people are the ones that were always willing to give a hand helping out and all. Now you can see how much help I have today. It's kind of disheartening.

"To me it's incomprehensible that someone would take that type of drastic action, you know? My way of handling a thing is if I got a beef with somebody, I'll kick their ass or they'll kick mine."

He scoffed at the idea of a conspiracy. "I've seen police in action before, and I've seen a lot of people in Illinois get loose because of overzealous police work. And I'm not saying this is overzealous police work, but it sure leads me to believe that it is. I don't believe it's any big conspiracy. No, I don't."

He also waved away suspicions about Norma Bondeson. "I suppose after you spent twenty-five years in the service and then came home, and then here and gone again, and stick to yourself, I suppose people would talk about ya, you know? That's my opinion. If you come and live in a house for a couple of weeks, and then you leave for a month, and then you come back for a couple of weeks, I suppose they're gonna say, 'What's she got going?'"

Doug, a full-blooded Swede, is not a member of GA, but the idea of Norma trying to take over the church, he says, is preposterous. "Nah! You don't know old Swedes very well if you think that," he said. "They're hardheaded and stubborn. You ain't gonna move them with a peavey. This is all speculation. Give me some proof. Give me some proof and then I'll believe it . . . Yeah, I'm not big on pointing fingers without any proof."

And so the organizers of the event tried to put on a positive face, knowing many visitors were more interested in the church and its troubles than the recipes for lutefisk and meatballs. They invited Henry Thomas, grandson of New Sweden's founder, William Widgery Thomas, and he accepted, after having missed the town's biggest celebration for more than a decade.

Sunday afternoon brought a happy surprise, when celebrants were read a letter from the mythical town of Lake Wobegon, Minnesota, with its bachelor farmers, potluck suppers, and solid Lutheran values. Author Garrison Keillor had been invited to come and lift the spirits of New Sweden. Instead he sent a letter from "Some of Us in Lake Wobegon."

As good Lutherans do, you are examining your consciences with a steel brush, and I beg you not to rub too hard and hurt yourselves. The setbacks in life come suddenly, whereas progress is slow, slow, slow. And when festivity and lightness do return to your hearts, it will be even lighter, as a result of all that's happened. You will be kinder, more loving, and funnier, if that is possible.

Keillor's words were a balm on bleeding spirits, a sweet remedy of hope. As Nancy Jepson Troy prepared her family for the trip back to Ohio, her young son Matteus spoke up. "Midsommar," the boy observed, "is thankfulness for the coming of light after the cold, dark winter."

Shabby Behavior

Several months after the poisoning, church members were horrified to learn that someone had placed a GA hymnal on eBay, trying to auction it off as a souvenir. "Arsenic Church Lutheran Book of Worship," read the listing, and if that wasn't offensive enough, the seller had set the minimum bid at five hundred dollars, plus another twenty-five for shipping. The church members thought it was shameful, and that it was probably that sleazy reporter who had been coming around trying to write a book. Anything for a buck, the almighty dollar.

At first, they asked Detective Millett to look into it, to find out if the reporter had done it. And what an attitude they got from him! He had said something like, "Do you want me to solve this murder, or chase after a frigging prayer book?" That is when Erica Grace volunteered to track it down. If the police wouldn't do their job, then Erica Grace would do it for them.

It didn't take Erica long. She logged on to eBay and recognized the E-mail address of the seller. It was not a reporter after all. It was one of Erica's best buddies—make that a "former" best buddy.

It was Doug McIntire, a smart, witty young man who had served on the church council and then left the area just before the poisoning to study for the ministry. He was also going through a divorce, and Erica had taken him under her wing. He had attended the pig roast with Erica and her friends, had enjoyed Easter dinner at her house, and celebrated her family members' birthdays. "Lois is like everyone's mom," he said. "'If you're coming over for lunch—you'll be staying for dinner. She'll have six home-made pies lined up. She won't make one; she'll make six and have a huge feast.'"

Why, Erica Grace had even babysat Doug's two kids when she was sick with a blood infection. And what did she get in return? A one-time friend trying to make money off the fact that her mother had almost died.

Erica made a photocopy of the eBay listing, brought it to the council, and with a heavy heart, revealed the disappointing news: The seller was not a reporter, but their very own Doug McIntire, the seemingly polite and respectful fellow for whom the church had thrown a farewell bash, and to whom the ladies of the church had given two hundred fifty dollars as a going-away gift.

Yes, sir, they had—and this was the thanks they got.

When her meeting with the council was over, Erica performed another unpleasant duty. She posted the eBay auction notice on the church bulletin board, with DOUG MCINTIRE scrawled across the page, for the entire congregation to see.

Erica had one last task before closing the matter: Send Doug an e-mail to say how very disappointed the church was in him, and to ask him to please return the hymnal (they had noticed, thank heavens, that nobody placed a bid). On a personal note, Erica Grace added how his shabby behavior had made her feel.

Not surprisingly, Doug did not respond.

Erica Grace was unstoppable. She made another plan.

This time, she would ambush Doug—online. She put his screen name on her Buddy List. And one day, it popped up. Erica confronted him.

"I am mad at you," she wrote, "and I want to know why you did this."

"You should be mad at me," Doug typed back. "But it isn't about the money. It's about the church. I've given up on it."

"But does that mean you can take advantage of the situation, the fact that my MOTHER almost DIED?" Erica demanded.

"Well, I would've been at church that Sunday, and I would've had my kids, and I would've died in front of my kids that night," Doug replied.

"The fact is you didn't," Erica wrote. "You weren't here; you DIDN'T drink the coffee; you DIDN'T almost die. So why are you TAKING ADVANTAGE of the CHURCH?"

"I can just picture the detectives going up there and asking what was wrong at the church," Doug replied, "and everyone saying there was no problem—even after somebody died."

"I ran it through in my mind," Doug said later. "I would have had my kids that weekend. I'm a caffeine junkie, and I would have had four or five cups of coffee. I'd have felt bad, but I'm the type that unless there's a bone jutting from the flesh, I don't go to the doctor. I would have gone home with the kids, feeling sick, and I lived way out in the woods. And I would have died horribly in front of my kids, leaving them scarred forever. It made me angry, more and more. Reid was a great guy. I loved Reid."

Doug paused for a moment before typing again: "Maybe somebody should ask Reid Morrill if there were problems in the church."

Screw the Pulpit to the Floor

Pastor Scottie Burkhalter arrived at Gustaf Adolph in 1998, fresh out of Lutheran Theological Seminary in Gettysburg, Pennsylvania. He had entered the clergy relatively late in life; after graduating from college in 1982, he spent fifteen years working in manufacturing jobs throughout the South. He showed up at GA at the age of thirty-eight, armed with a Master of Divinity degree and completely unprepared for the firing squad he was about to face.

The first time Pastor Scottie delivered a sermon, it was received with openmouthed astonishment. Traditionally, GA pastors had stood in the pulpit, delivering their sermons in somber, measured tones. A South Carolina native, Pastor Scottie was a dyed-in-the-wool Southern boy, and his lively evangelism was an embarrassing spectacle to this taciturn Yankee flock.

"They had to screw the pulpit to the floor." Lester Beaupre breaks into laughter at the memory. "He'd get up there, and he'd be hopping around from left to right, all excited, and the thing would start to wobble—they had to screw it down to the floor. If you ever go up to the pulpit and take a look at the base, you'll see black drywall screws all the way through to the floor."

"He was a young minister, just out of seminary—probably not the best choice for this particular congregation," said Debbie Blanchette. "He was emotional, kind of sappy sometimes. You know what, though? That was him. I loved him."

"He had this Lutheran-Baptist blend going," Doug McIntire said. "He was very energetic. He moved around a lot; he did not like preaching from the pulpit. He had a wireless mike, and he walked up and down the aisle. That really freaked them out. Old Swedish Lutherans—it was hilarious. I would watch them; Scottie would walk down past them, and they would not turn their heads. Like it was some sort of unspoken sin to turn your head and follow the man. Norma didn't like it because she said it gave her headaches."

Omar Lagasse, a member of GA for thirty-seven years, said Norma was "in that bunch that criticized" Pastor Scottie.

"One Sunday," Omar recalled, "Pastor Scottie said, 'When I'm saying something, if you want to say, "Amen," it's all right to say that. Or if you want to say, "Praise the Lord," it's all right to say that out loud.' And Norma said, 'If anybody sits alongside of me and says that, I'm sure not going to be here.'

"Well, what do you go to church for? You go to praise the Lord. God is good; he's good all the time."

"He came from a Baptist background and then became a Lutheran because he liked the doctrine and the theology," Debbie explained. "We don't do altar calls in the Lutheran church, and he gave an altar call, which is when you come forward and profess your faith in Christ. That's a little uncomfortable for us. And I'm thinking, oh, God, this isn't gonna work. You're going to be in hot water."

During the altar call, Debbie said, "Some brave wonderful soul came forward, and I thought, that's great. And if I hadn't been so, kind of shy, I probably would've gone too."

"It probably made some people uncomfortable," Lester said, "because he was happy, and with certain people in that church, if you were happy, you weren't with the program. And, of course, they weren't really used to having a guy stand up in front of them and say, 'Hey, good morning, y'all!' "

Despite the complaints about his offbeat approach, GA church attendance shot up, from an average sixty-three worshipers each Sunday to eighty during the first year Pastor Scottie was there.

"He was a real, real nice pastor," said Omar. "What a nice man; he was a jewel. He was great with everybody. I'm blind, and a pin came out of my tractor. And I was lying on my back on the grass, and I was trying to get that pin back in there, and I just couldn't get it back in there. And Pastor Scottie drove in the dooryard, and he offered to lay down there and put that pin in for me. And I said, 'No, that's all right, I'll get it sometime.' And he reached in his pocket and he had a little gold cross in his pocket. He said, 'I've been carrying this since I was a kid, and I want to give this to you for luck.' And he gave me that cross, and I hung on to that. I laid on my back, and that pin went in there; you'd think it fell in. It went in just like nuttin'."

Pastor Scottie and his wife, Myra, lived in the parsonage next to the church with their five children.

"We just looked at it as an adventure," Myra later recalled in her soft, lilting Southern accent. "It was beautiful. Going to the small school, it was great. Mrs. Landeen, who is the cook at the New Sweden School, she cooked everything homemade—yes—everything they got. If they had mashed potatoes, she peeled every potato and had mashed potatoes for this school. Shepherd's pie, it was great. And that's the kind of little school it was. My kids don't like their lunch now; they got spoiled."

Eldredge Palmer, a social studies teacher, knew the Burkhalter children in school, and had only praise for the entire family. "He had a different approach, he was upbeat," Eldredge said, speaking of Pastor Scottie. "I really liked him, and I liked his kids. You could tell they were well brought up; they were super kids. His oldest daughter, Elizabeth, was a sweetheart; she had a beautiful singing voice. She was one of the top singers in the school choir."

Despite their Southern upbringing, the Burkhalters got into the spirit of Maine's cold winter lifestyle and the small-town pleasures of New Sweden.

"We all had skis," Myra said, "and they would come and make a little track around Reid Morrill's house, through there where Ainar Gustafson used to live. Reid was a sweet man, he and Ellie. They always wanted the kids to come over at Halloween; they always had a little Halloween bag for them. She'd call and have the kids come over. He was on the property committee, and he'd come over and do little odd things in the house for us, he and Ralph. They were sweet guys."

In April 2001, after almost three years at GA, Pastor Scottie abruptly resigned. In a letter to the synod, he said that he and Myra wanted to be closer to their families down south. Ironically, Pastor Scottie had become very popular; enrollment at GA not only shot up by a third during his first year—it stayed that way the entire time he was there. When he quit, some members were so upset that they complained to the synod that he had been tormented, abused, and harassed out of the church by a small group of middle-aged thugs who always wanted things their own way.

Omar remembers an incident where "somebody was sassin' the pastor in that little office we had in the church, and she hollered so hard she woke the kids up in the parsonage. She was yellin' about his sermon was too long."

"Fran yelled at him once," said Debbie Blanchette. "My daughter Christy was there; I don't know what it was about. And then there was another time that Fran had gone over to the parsonage. She opened up the door to the parsonage and started yelling at him in his own house. And the kids were there in the living room, and she was saying some pretty horrible things, and he just plain asked her to leave. And she wouldn't leave, and he said, 'You need to leave.' He told me after he resigned, and I said, 'Oh my God, why didn't you tell us this? That's harassment, downright harassment.' But by that time he had started to look elsewhere."

Fran also did not want the pastor to be involved with the Sunday school, of which she was superintendent, according to Debbie.

"This was our pastor," said Debbie. "We wanted him to come to Sunday school. And Fran made it very evident to him that he was not welcome in Sunday school. She just didn't like his mannerism, and she thought he was having too much control over the council."

Money was also a thorny issue at the church. Omar said the congregation voted at an annual meeting to raise Pastor Scottie's annual salary by a thousand dollars. "And some of them didn't think we could afford it, and they got into fights together, and they'd bunch up, you know, a bunch here and a bunch there, and they talked about it," he said. "And we voted on it again, and they voted to give it to him anyway. And Pastor Scottie said, 'If people are mad about this, then I won't take the thousand dollars.' That's how nice a guy he was."

During one debate about the pastor's salary, Doug recalled, "Barbara Margeson stood up and said, 'If we're going to do this we need to act in faith that God will provide.' She was the only one who brought up anything faith based in the argument. I was so struck."

Pastor Scottie had zero authority at Gustaf Adolph, according to Doug: "Every other place I've been, the council and the pastor worked together, where the pastor is seen like the mayor of the town and the council. At GA the pastor is supposed to be a pawn of the council. The pastor is supposed to keep his mouth shut and do what he's told."

Certain church members had even less regard for the synod, according to Doug. "They referred to the synod as 'those people'—those people down there that don't know what they're doing," he said. "Every other church I've been to, the synod is the organization, they're the people who are going to help us, and they're the people we go to with questions. Up there, they are the enemy."

Pastor Scottie made a special effort to involve the kids in church activities. In the summertime, someone would lend him a van, and he'd take a group of kids to Camp Calumet, a Lutheran camp in New Hampshire. His goal was to have all the kids of the church go to Calumet.

"He had a large involvement with Camp Calumet, which they didn't like," Doug said. "Fran would say, 'We're paying his salary. We're paying his salary to be here, not Camp Calumet.' Fran was ringleader in a lot of ways. She kicked up the dust a lot."

Shortly after Pastor Scottie arrived at GA, Barbara Margeson was diagnosed with terminal cancer. Omar remembers attending a service after she got the news: "When Pastor Scottie came down off the pulpit, I remember walking down the aisle, and I went down front, and Barb was sitting there with a pillow on her back. I laid my hands on his shoulder, and I said, 'You know, we ought to have a special prayer for Barb.'

"So I said what I wanted to say, and Pastor Scottie—he prayed. When he got done, people were crying; everybody felt bad; Barb was a good person. And she laid her hands on my heart while I was praying. And the next time we went to church, she said, 'I know that I'm not healed, but I feel so much peace, I just can't explain it.' I'll never forget that."

"She had planned her own funeral," remembered Debbie, "and it was probably about an hour and a half long—Pastor Scottie was following her wishes. And Julie yelled at him. He told me this after he resigned. He said he was outside walking back to the parsonage, and he said, 'Julie yelled at me. She yelled at me, wanting to know why on earth I had ever allowed the service to go on like that.' "

Debbie said she asked Pastor Scottie if Julie knew that Barb had planned it herself. "He said, 'Oh, I couldn't get a word in edgewise.' "

"She screamed at him even after he explained that Barb knew she was dying and had planned her own funeral," Doug said. "Barb was this incredible woman, and she loved him. So, of course, Scottie was devastated."

"That," said Debbie, "was probably the beginning of the end."

After Pastor Scottie left, church attendance plummeted to its lowest levels ever.

"You know, he wasn't for just certain people; he was for everybody," Omar said. "In the church, there is a whole bunch of pastors' pictures hanging on the wall, a big bunch. When Pastor Scottie came he said to my wife, 'How come there's been so many pastors in this church?' And she said, 'Just give it a few weeks, and you'll find out.' He did."

"Pastor Scottie was very careful not to name names," Doug said, "but he tried warning me before he left. 'Don't let this place beat you up,' he said. 'Let stuff roll off your back. Be careful.'"

"I know Scottie was probably quite a bit more conservative in his beliefs than the local people," said Eldredge Palmer. "I am, too. Talking to him, we seemed to be on the same page—we're fundamentalist. I was not aware that anything was wrong. He never alluded to that too much, but I always felt probably something happened and that's why he left."

Other people had no doubt about the reasons for Scottie's departure. The very mention of Pastor Scottie's experience at GA got Lanie Wilson all riled up. "I'll tell you why he left. Pastor Burkhalter left because there were a select few people that gave him too much of a hard time."

Lanie had been a member of GA for many years, but she left the church when Burkhalter resigned, and three years later, she was still steaming. "There were a few people that gave Pastor Scottie a real, real hard time," she said. "In fact, they didn't respect him and made it very difficult for him. So much so that he didn't have to put up with that foolishness and found another church and left. We were pleased for him, but very sad that he left.

"He is a fine gentleman—a fine, fine gentleman. I liked everything about him. He was, in my mind, the best pastor we ever had. He could give a good sermon. He was wonderful with youth. He built that church up. Sunday school tripled in the first year he was there. He made it interesting; he made it come alive . . . . He was so kind and so thoughtful and so loving, you know, just a great guy.

"The synod is in Massachusetts, and out of sight, out of mind. And they don't know what goes on up here unless someone tells them. I thought someone writing a letter to the synod would prompt them to look into it. But they came up, and they visited us and questioned us, but nothing was really done about it. These people were allowed to do the preaching. And it went on, and then this bad thing happened.

"You see, there are people who won't be happy in heaven. If they're not in charge, they boycott. There are those few people that do. And the congregation wasn't that big. So many people say they're Lutherans, but they go to church once a year. If you'd had a bigger congregation, those few people could have been overridden.

"You go to school to be a writer, an attorney, or whatever your field may be. Who am I to go to you and say, 'You don't know how to write; I can do better.' I'm a layperson; I have no clue. Well, that's exactly what they were doing. They made it hard for him in every manner they could. If you tried to help him, then you were a culprit as well. You put up with that so long, and you can't handle that anymore; and therefore, he left. After that, they ran the church, and that's what they wanted.

"I firmly believe that Jesus Christ couldn't please them. It is so frustrating. It's no fun. They were down on him so much that he couldn't even breathe right.

"For example, on his sermons, if he went five minutes over, they called him on the carpet; they said he was too long-winded. They'd sass him. And the sad part of it was, then after church they always had refreshments—coffee, the famous coffee—and they could sit there for an hour at a time and chew the fat, and that was all right.

"Whenever the bishop came up, he would ask, 'What are you looking for in a new pastor?' And they would say, 'Somebody good with youth.' Well, holy fright, how much more did they have than Pastor Scottie? The man was doing everything they were looking for, but they were too damn blind to see. They were focused on one thing, and that was trying to make it so hard for him that he would leave.

"He could not win—he could not win. I do know of an incident that Fran Ruggles yelled at him, and the family was at home, and they heard her yelling at him. It didn't matter what he did. She just all the time was riveting at him. She probably was the worst one of all.

"How would a person like to go and sit there and listen to these jackasses present the sermon to you? It just stands to reason. Here you have people who've been so very difficult, and then they can stand in the pulpit and tell you how to live. It's just not right. So therefore, you can't blame anyone for not attending, and that's why their attendance is down. They seem to feel they're right and we're wrong.

"The Fishers wanted to run the show. And the Ruggles; let's see, who else? Julie Adler. I would say that's it: Adler, Fisher, Fran Ruggles. Fran is a native of the area, was in the military for quite a while with her husband, then she came back to New Sweden.

"They'd start to dislike someone—you don't have to do anything wrong. One person dislikes them, that's too bad, they just follow suit. And no matter what Pastor Scottie tried, they didn't want it to work. That's why he left. They may not tell you that, but it is. How would you like to work in a place where people are picking on you and you're in a fishbowl? You don't want to stay there. Life is too short. He didn't start off on the wrong foot. They just were so sweet to him, and then all of a sudden, it just went the other way.

But that's the way they are. They get tired of you, and they send you away.

"They are tight with each other. If you alienate one, if you do something to someone that they don't like, then they all turn against you. Just like a bunch of kids. For example, if I don't like Mary, well, that means all my family would say, 'I don't like Mary.' This is gospel truth. They're not open-minded at all, and they will say, 'Whose side am I on?' And then proceed from there. It's very true. That's disheartening, because it's not right. If you follow your own beliefs, and you don't follow them, you're a bad guy, not a good guy."

After Pastor Scottie left Gustaf Adolph, Associate Bishop Hans Arneson traveled to New Sweden to meet with the church council.

"I sat there at the meeting with Hans and the rest of the council," Doug McIntire recalled. "He's very direct, very straightforward. He's like, 'So, guys, what happened? What was the problem? And they all sat around that table with these deer-in-the-headlight looks—me, Herman, Ralph, Reid, Karla, Dick, Fran, Janet, and/or Shirley. But everyone around the table was like, 'I wasn't aware there was a problem. I thought he was moving to be closer to his family—that's what he said in his resignation letter.'

"I sat there and I leaned back and looked at them like they all had another head growing. I said, 'Guys, he left because of problems he was having with us.' And I had a big target painted on me; I just felt eyes drilling through me. A lot of people started squirming in their chairs."

After his meeting with the church council, Hans Arneson and two other synod associates spent three days at Gustaf Adolph, interviewing members about conflicts within the church. Several months later, Arneson issued a report describing "an overall spirit of discontent, suspicion, and control."

"It's all power struggles," Doug observed. "Think about this small church and the people that go to it in New Sweden, Maine. You have people who in their own lives have no power—none. They're farmers; they work at a convenience store. These are people who are at the bottom of the food chain really, as far as being powerful and feeling powerful themselves. Suddenly you're in this small church where there aren't enough people to get the job done; you're important. So suddenly your identity is wrapped around your position in this church. And that's why the few people that run the church are there all the time and they're so invested in it."

Arneson's report also mentioned "rampant power plays" at the church, and said many members felt the "power base" within the congregation was the Worship and Music Committee. It consisted of Karla and Herman Fisher, Julie Adler, and her sister, Fran Ruggles. They were responsible for setting up the altar and scheduling the lay minister and liturgist each week.

"They did have the power," Doug said. "They had the power when Scottie was there, just by default. They were the ones who did most of the chores around the church. Herman worked a lot of maintenance on the parsonage and on the church."

In addition to her committee duties, Karla also served as choir director and organist. "That takes quite a bit of time," Doug said. "She gathered all the music information; then, of course, she had to learn it, get it down pat so that she could rehearse with the choir once a week."

Despite that, Karla rarely accepted the stipend to which she was entitled. "It was minuscule; I don't even think it was a hundred dollars a month," Doug said. "It was really very little, but it accumulated over a long period of time."

Once Doug announced his intention to enroll in seminary, Pastor Scottie began offering him chances to act as lay minister, so he could get up in the pulpit and speak. But after Scottie left, Doug's rotation got cut by Worship and Music. "I was no longer on the schedule," Doug said. "Herman replaced me. Karla had a large role in that. I think I was infringing upon their power base.

"It came down to their own will, more or less—Herman and Karla getting together and putting together a schedule. I did as I was told. I felt I was offering service to the church; I was working for the church, and I didn't want to be like 'I'm not getting my due,' because that sounded way too self-centered. I think Herman's involvement in the church, in general, was just as deep as Karla's. I don't think he was just tagging along. I think their agendas interlaced. They were a lot of the driving force behind the people who wanted it done their way."

Arneson did not limit his admonitions to the "power base." He also issued a warning to those who would put heritage before faith: "The Swedish identity was more clearly expressed than the Christian identity . . . and the mission of Christ in the world. The orientation of the congregation [is] toward the past and the church's historical roots, and not toward the future. This identity . . . is the orientation of a dying church."

That statement, one investigator would later say, may be part of what triggered the poisoning. Others were intrigued by a quote Arneson repeated, saying it came from a "wise person" he did not name: "We need to be the church in practice and not just in theory. There needs to be a cleansing.

"That," Arneson wrote, "is a fine summary."

It Just Kept Boiling

At first glance, there seemed to be a unanimously agreed-upon view of Danny Bondeson: helpful, cheerful, friendly, a little bit shy, wouldn't hurt a fly. These impressions, of course, were superficial, and nobody seems to have known Danny well enough to have been his close friend or confidante during the years immediately preceding his death. In New Sweden, Danny was considered the salt of the earth, and if he was troubled, his neighbors and friends failed to notice.

Eldredge Palmer was a long-distance runner who became acquainted with Danny during the 1980s and early 1990s, when the two men traveled to races and marathons throughout the region. By 2003, Eldredge had given up competitive running and only saw Danny in passing. He could also see that something wasn't right.

"I did notice he changed quite a lot in the last few years," Eldredge said. "I used to see him when he'd substitute teach; he'd come to the school where I taught. And I noticed quite a change in him. He didn't take care of himself as well; he didn't dress well. I was talking to my daughter about it. She was saying, boy, she had a real big crush on Danny, because she'd go to the races with me sometimes. She was a lot younger than him—she's only thirty-seven now—but she was saying how she had a crush on him and what a neat-looking guy he was. He kept himself very clean and neat."

It was not only Danny's hygiene that suggested something was amiss.

"He was a little different, and people made fun of him," said Eldredge. "We used him really bad in that respect, behind his back. I think he felt that; I think he knew that. I think he really, really knew that, and it bothered him."

The perception of Danny as the butt of jokes and the object of mockery is consistent with investigators' interpretations of his suicide note—that he thought certain council members were "playing tricks" on him. It also jibes with what detectives heard about his alleged mistreatment by Carl. Danny might have been more than "a little different," as Eldredge kindly put it. He might have been mentally ill.

"Danny had emotional problems people didn't realize," observed longtime Gustaf Adolph member Sally Sandstrom. "Taking care of his father, his father being sickly, and then going to the nursing home and taking care of sick people again really didn't do him any good. Before, he was very involved in the church. I think it takes a toll on a person after a while, staying with a sick person day in and day out. He drove his father everywhere; he took care of his father; he was with him all the time. And I think that took a toll on him, not getting out with people his own age, not living his own life, putting his own life on hold.

"It all started over a communion table, because certain people in the church didn't want the communion table, and it probably just boiled and boiled on him. There were certain things they tried to do in the church, and I think it just kept boiling. You can only take so much sometimes."

But if Danny did not attend church, as most people said, why would he crack over petty church issues?

"Dan still went to that church; I'm sure of that," said

Lanie Wilson. "It was just that he probably didn't attend as often as people would've liked him to attend. He had a job to do. Dan volunteered to work on weekends because he got more pay. If you're working at the nursing home over the weekend, it's pretty hard to attend church. The church was still very important to him."

According to Eldredge, the church was an important social outlet for Danny. "He and his father, any time the church had an activity going on, they'd be there," Eldredge said. "If you had a supper or special people there or something, they'd show up. Like I said, I thought Danny had changed quite a bit, and I saw some things in him. I never could feel he probably would do [the poisoning] himself if he didn't have an influence there that encouraged him a little bit, maybe. I really don't know because you don't know what snaps in somebody's head, but I just really couldn't see Danny being that type of person; yet I have seen signs where he could get very upset over things.

"I don't like to put him down because he was very friendly to me," Eldredge said. "But another thing I noticed, one time we got into a discussion on politics and he really got livid. I'm an ultraconservative, and he was on the other end, which I didn't realize. I just made a few statements, and he really exploded."

"He worked at the school, and he helped Carl," said Lanie. "When you're not thinking and you're overtired, it's pretty hard. It could've been sleep deprivation. You don't think straight. You do things when you're not one hundred percent, and you wonder why. And I firmly believe that Dan certainly would not have wanted to hurt anyone; he was a good guy. He worked so hard, and he wanted to help everybody and do good for everybody, and he just had many different jobs going, and he worked day and night. He probably thought he was going to do this to scare a few people and just hurt their belly as much as they were hurting him."

Hound Dogs and Coyotes

Some time after the poisoning, Lt. Dennis Appleton was asked by a reporter if Daniel Bondeson was an angry man. "There's no real indication of that," he replied. Had he met Wendell Hudson, however, his answer might have been different.

Wendell is a hunter and trapper from Mapleton, not far from New Sweden. He met Daniel Bondeson in the late 1990s, when he asked permission to hunt on Daniel's property using hound dogs. The story he tells reveals a side of Daniel Bondeson that many people never saw.

"I actually asked him right outright, 'Can I hunt on your property?' And he goes, 'Well, I don't care if you hunt here. I don't want them dogs chasin' my cows.' I said, 'Well, they ain't gonna chase no cows.' And he goes, 'Well, go ahead, but I don't really like it.' I didn't want him to shoot my dogs or get into no row over that. So that was the first year.

"And the next year we come back, huntin' some bears, and pretty soon we run into his brother Pete, and Pete stopped me and he wanted to know if I'd run the coyotes and get 'em away from his barn and his pigs. So me and some other guys from downstate put the hound dogs on two coyotes, and run 'em down towards Blackstone Siding. And the coyotes came back on the Bondeson Road, and they crossed the road. We seen one cross the road, and when we went down to put some dogs on it, the other one came out in the road, and we run over it by accident.

"But anyway, the one that was wild and loose, he went just beyond the house. There's a potata house there that sets in the ground; the top of it's just above the ground, and the coyote tried to get in the back side, and we have collars for the dogs so we can find them. So we got a reading on the dogs, and we went down there. One of the guys I was with radioed me. He said, 'The dogs got the coyote behind this guy's potata house; he's trying to get in the potata house.'

"So I went down, and boy when Danny came out, *whew!* He was rippin' mad. He wanted to fight. He didn't care whether the coyote ate Pete's pigs or not. He just didn't want us to take the coyote on his property, which we had no power over, because the coyote can go where he wants.

"But what I remember most is his veins were sticking out in his neck, and his fist was clenched, and he was going to poke somebody in the nose. And the two other guys with me, they grabbed the coyote by the tail and drug him up on the road. The dogs was fightin' with him, and the coyote bit one of the dogs right in the mouth, on top of the roof of his mouth, and the blood was squirtin' all over the snow, and all over the potata house. And then he made us clean off the potata house with rags, and take a shovel and shovel all the bloody snow up on the road. And he wouldn't let us use his rags or his shovel. We had to find our own. That's how mad he was.

"And I just, I didn't want to start no fight 'cause I felt like I was at a disadvantage due to the fact that we was on his property, so I said, 'Well, whatever you tell us to do, we'll do it.' So we did. We found our own rags and we found a shovel, and we cleaned it up.

"Another incident was when I was just settin' on the grass around the corner there on the Margison Road. Dan drove up and down the road, real slow, real slow, five miles an hour. Down the road, back the road, and I could see him when he come up, I see him. I didn't know if he's lookin' for somethin', a cow got out, or something. He just glared at me, and then the next time, about the third trip by—I was just settin' beside the road—just settin' there, and he pulled right up and started sassin' me. He said, 'You're huntin' down with the dogs again.' So I just let him sass me, and finally I asked him, I asked him point blank: 'Look, what is it? What is it I've done? I serve God, and I know that there can be confrontations between two people that believe in God. What have I done to you? Let's take care of this thing, 'cause I don't have no hard feelings against you, and I don't know what I've done to you. Tell me.' And he says, 'You threw a bunch of garbage on Pete's land.' And I said, 'I absolutely—you can talk to my friends—I disdain garbage. Even with a bunch of guys, I see 'em drop a bottle or a piece of paper, I'll get right out and pick it up myself. I'll tell them about it, and if they don't want to, I'll pick it up myself. So I know for a fact it wasn't me.' But he was trying to accuse me of something, so I just said, 'Well, it wasn't me that did that.' He says, 'Oh, yes it was, oh, yes it was, I saw your pickup on the road that day.' I said, 'Well, you didn't see me throw it out, didja?' He said, 'No, but I know it was you.' I said, 'Well, how do you know it was me?' I tried to talk to him, but he was beyond reason. All I can figure is he might not like the method of the hound dogs chasing the coyote.

"One woman I know, she didn't like hunting. She definitely was against it. But all of a sudden the coyotes come in, and killed the mother cat and killed her kitten. And she called me on the phone, wanted to know if I'd go hunt 'em, and I said, 'No.' I said, 'I'm not gonna hunt 'em. I wanna tell you, just point blank, that the coyote did that naturally; he killed your cats, and now you don't like the coyote because he did it. But before he did that, you didn't want me to hunt the coyotes. So I'm not gonna go down that road. I'm not comin' over.'

"But I think what he saw was the blood, and the dogs barkin' at the coyote, and then fightin' with the coyote, and I think maybe he was havin' a bad day, I don't know.

"The last time I saw him was when I was invited to a party over there at the church, to sing and play the guitar. And I did, and I remember he was there with his father. And I approached him to try to talk to him, and he didn't wanna talk. He didn't want to acknowledge me, even in a church. I thought, well, that's not good because you would think in a church you'd want to put things behind you and go on with something. But I remember filing it away in my mind. I thought, my land, this man is really bitter about something. I don't know what it was. He never told me."

Erica's Coup

"I've got to keep the pot stirred; I've got to keep her going."
Erica wore a satisfied smile as she spoke. She had scored a
major victory at the annual congregational meeting.
Norma Bondeson had lost her position as Sunday school
superintendent. Erica and her aunt Penny Anderson would
be officially in charge. If that didn't drive Norma crazy, Erica would see to it that something else would. Erica believed that Norma knew a lot about the poisoning and that
eventually, if she could be brought to the breaking point,
she would tell everything she knew. "I've got to keep the
stew going," she said, "because if I just let it go, she'll
never crack. I've got to build up to it. And that's what I've
been doing, and I've got her just about where I want her."

According to Erica, Norma had been politely asked to
step down as Sunday school superintendent because some
of the parents did not trust her, and when she refused to
quit, they asked Erica to stay and keep an eye on her.
"There were about eight or nine kids who weren't allowed
to go to Sunday school unless I was there," Erica said.

"That's when I said, you know what? It's time for me to take over."

It also seemed to Erica that Sally Sandstrom, who had always been Norma's ally, had switched sides. "Sally was scared of Norma, because Norma was in charge of Sunday school," Erica explained.

Sally Sandstrom, however, offered a different version of what happened.

"I'm sorry to say there was a proposal to get Norma out of being superintendent of Sunday school," Sally said. "That campaign was a whole plunge to get Norma out of there, that's all. I think Erica was put up by Julie and Fran and other ladies to do it. They pretty much pushed her in that direction. I think she has her own set of problems, and then these older ladies all became her friends, and she needed friends. I think she was taken in by that."

Sally said it is not true that parents were concerned about leaving their children at Sunday school with Norma in charge.

"Norma did a very good job at Sunday school. She always knew all the lessons beforehand. She used *The Little Red Book.* We did the Apostles' Creed. And she always knew what lesson we were on, and gave a little talk about the lesson. She went through the steps of Lent. Now the children don't get that. She knew how to delegate work, how to plan and make things happen, and how to go about things to make things happen. Norma knew how to set up programs and get everything organized. She'd teach when somebody wasn't there. She was a very good Sunday school superintendent.

"They gave Norma such a hard time at Christian Ed meetings. It was really bad. She got two CD players. And she didn't ask permission, but we needed the CD players because Karla refused to play the piano anymore at the Sunday school. So we needed someone to buy music, so Norma went out and bought CD players with her own money and asked to be reimbursed from the Sunday school fund. And they just wouldn't give up on her: 'Well, when we buy something we have to ask permission.' They just wouldn't let up. Fran is stubborn and very rude. She's very, very rude. She has her own way, and that's the only way, and you know, it's so sad to be that way. It really is. She's quite bad. I don't know if she realizes she's doing that or not. Now Fran doesn't come to any more Christian Ed meetings because Norma's gone. She served her purpose, you know? It's sad."

Erica launched her get-rid-of-Norma campaign by attending every Sunday school session after the poisoning. Once, Norma asked Erica if she was going to help out with the lessons.

"No, I'm not prepared," Erica informed her.

"Well, you can go home," Norma replied.

Erica did not go home. She stayed and watched Norma like a hawk.

On another Sunday, Norma asked Erica what she was doing there. "I have to watch you," Erica said. "I have to keep an eye on you and make sure you don't hurt these kids."

"Norma was so angry that her face went white," Erica said later, pleased.

The ballot at the 2004 congregational meeting offered two choices for co-superintendents: Erica Anderson and Penny Anderson, or Norma Bondeson and Debbie Blanchette. Debbie's candidacy made Erica all the more determined to win. She believed Debbie had been trying underhanded things at the church and that Debbie and Norma were thick as thieves.

Erica recalled an incident when the associate bishop, Hans Arneson, came up for a visit just a couple of months earlier. "Okay, this is petty," Erica said, "but Debbie lied, and I found out. When Arneson came up, Justin Fisher was supposed to take him for a snowmobile ride. It was all planned. Karla had made the arrangements. Justin was all excited because he was going to take the guy who had baptized his child on a snowmobile ride. Justin doesn't get excited about much, but this kid was just thrilled. And Friday morning Arneson got an e-mail from Debbie that said, 'Something's come up; I know Justin was going to take you for a ride, but something came up and he won't be able to, so my husband, Emery, will take you.' Now, Justin doesn't talk to Debbie, can't stand Debbie, doesn't like Emery, and doesn't like their kids, so how would she know something came up with Justin? Anyway, Arneson took that as truth and went for a ride with Emery. Justin sat all day Saturday waiting to take Arneson for a ride. He didn't even go with his wife to have his child's picture taken."

Debbie tells it differently: "Herman announced in church that Pastor Arneson was coming and bringing someone. And he said, 'Pastor Arneson had never gone for a sled ride, and he would like to go for a sled ride, and would anybody volunteer?' I raised my hand and said, 'I would love to take him for a ride, or Emery will take him for a ride.' Then I put my hand down. Then Pastor Arneson e-mailed me, 'We're coming Friday afternoon.' And I said, 'Would you like to come and have supper with us?' And he said, 'I'm bringing someone with me.' I wrote back and said, 'He or she is welcome to come, too. We'd love to have you, and Emery or Josh will take you for a sled ride.' And he never said Justin was going to do it."

Erica did not buy Debbie's story. She was sure Debbie wanted the power in the church and was trying to take over, little by little. For example, Erica said, Debbie took over confirmation instruction and then tried to pull a fast one by only teaching two Sundays instead of four.

"Debbie said she would meet every Sunday in the Sunday school," Erica explained, "and I found out the truth. She's only teaching confirmation twice a month instead of four times a month. The other two Sundays, she made it a regular Sunday school class; and if that isn't bad enough, she has somebody else teaching those other two Sundays! So she's only teaching half of what she's supposed to, for half the time she's supposed to. This is not kosher. I attended confirmation classes for three years."

Hearing this, Debbie Blanchette rolled her eyes. "Norma asked Laurie Spooner and me last fall if we would teach Sunday school," she recalled. "Norma said to me, 'You know, I'm not a very good person working with kids.' She's more of an adult person, she said. That's not her thing, which is fine. She knows her strengths and weaknesses.

"And then confirmation came up, and I said, 'Who's going to take confirmation?' I was hoping Pastor Morgan would do it, but then he resigned. And then I said, 'Sunday School is just as important as confirmation; I'm a teacher, and I can teach forty-five minutes of confirmation if somebody would teach the Sunday school part.' And so Laurie was teaching Sunday school, and I ended up teaching two Sundays of confirmation."

Still, Erica would have none of Debbie's explanations. "She's going down for that bullshit she pulled," she vowed. Erica was not accusing Debbie of being involved in the poisoning, but she was sure she knew something about it because Debbie and Norma were friends. "Norma's got Debbie in so deep it's not funny," Erica said. "It's not that Janet and Shirley and all them fall behind Norma a hundred percent—it's that they believe in Debbie. So now I'm going after Debbie, too."

True to her word, Erica caused Debbie some headaches. "We had this council meeting the first of February," Debbie recalled. "Erica comes in—she's not on the council—she comes in and sits down. What had happened was, I had some money in a fund for camp. There had been money set aside for camp, and there was something like twenty-four dollars left in it on the first of July. In December I had closed it, so when I went to do my statement, of course I couldn't find the July or August statement anywhere, and the account was three dollars short out of twenty-four dollars. Since they were supposed to audit, I had called the bank that afternoon and said, 'Can you tell me how much interest?' There was one penny interest for both July and

August, and it was missing that three dollars. So I sent it in like that.

"The auditing committee, which was Erica and Wanda Conroy and Janet Erickson, audited the books. Wanda called me and said, 'Debbie, your books don't balance.' I said, 'I know; I don't know what happened to the three dollars,' blah blah blah. So she says, 'And you're missing two statements.' I said, 'I did call the bank; the interest is a penny for July and August. With the three dollars, the only thing I can think is I think I made out a money order to pay back Norma for going to Camp Calumet. So that's probably where that three dollars is. That's the only thing I can think of.' Wanda said, 'Okay, not a problem.' So they corrected it in our annual report. We had our annual meeting, nobody said boo to me about it; it was corrected by the auditing committee. So at the annual meeting, Wanda said, 'I want to resign because I have two little kids and I really don't have time to do it.' And Herman said, 'We can't really do it until the first council meeting; then you can resign.'

"So we had our council meeting and Erica's there. She passes a letter to the secretary, Arline, and she says, 'This is from Wanda.' Arline says, 'Oh, it's her letter of resignation.' So Arline reads it out loud without having a chance to read it first: 'I resign from the auditing committee, and I want to say something about Debbie's budget. I spent an awful lot of time . . .'

"And I'm thinking, I know where this comes from. So Shirley looked at me, and Erica said, 'We took a lot of time working over this.' And I thought, *Bullshit you did*. I was embarrassed, and also very, very angry. I ended up taking Louise home, and I stopped at Shirley and Janet's before I went home. And I said, 'Janet, you were there, did that take you a long time?' She said, 'Oh, no, Debbie.'

"It came from Erica. She and Wanda are really good friends. Arline called a couple of days later, and she said, 'Debbie, I just want you to know that was not called for.' And I said, 'Arline, look at where it came from. I know where it came from.'"

For Erica, besides getting rid of Norma, becoming superintendent of the Sunday school had another benefit: She would be teaching Finn occasionally, and she was pretty sure he knew something. She and a few other people thought it was oddly coincidental that Finn just happened to be sick on the day of the poisoning and the whole week before that. Even one of the detectives suspected Finn, and he had come to Erica for her opinion on the matter.

"He asked me if I thought Finn was involved, and I said, 'I don't know. I won't tell you deep down in my heart if I really believe it, because it's a kid, and when it comes to kids, I'm sorry; I just love kids.'"

But Erica had to admit that Finn was with Norma all the time, and he did seem a little different recently. "I would never have had a problem with Finn before the poisoning," she said. "He was a very good kid, but then after the poisoning, he got very cocky and whatnot. I used to think of him as an average, everyday kid. But now his attitude is different—kind of more like his father and more like Norma."

Erica had also noticed that when she taught Finn in Sunday school, he was better behaved than when Norma taught him. "I taught him this past Sunday," she said, "and that kid had so much fun. He was the Finn I used to know. I let him pick the first song, and he was excited because I let him pick it. And we sang the song that he wanted, and he was laughing, having a blast, and I'd never seen this kid this happy when Norma was doing Sunday school.

"A lot of people ask me, 'Well, do you think Finn was poisoned?' I don't know, and unless the police can show me it, I don't even want to say anything about that."

The police never showed Erica a shred of evidence that Finn was involved in the poisoning, nor did anyone else. Yet her imagination cranked out dramatic scenarios with Finn as a central character. For example, after having Finn in class, she could go up to Norma and say something to scare her; to make her believe that Finn had ratted her out. "I could fit it up perfect," Erica explained. "I could go up to her and say, 'I just found out something. I know what you're taking to your grave.' Boom. Is she going to come after me? If she comes after me, she has a suit on her hands because I'm never alone. If she comes after me, somebody else is going to be there. And I will, I'll call the nearest cop I can get and have her arrested, just enough to get her name out in the paper."

Sally Sandstrom gives little credence to Erica's claims. "You have to watch Erica." She sighed. "Because, sometimes you don't know whether she's telling the truth or not telling the truth. And people like that I usually stand back from."

Erica said the Sunday school went back to full enrollment after she and Penny Anderson took over. According to Karla, "There wouldn't be a Sunday school if it weren't for Erica."

Banjo Boy

There is a widely accepted local belief that Erica's parents, Carl and Lois Anderson, are first cousins. They are not, but the claim has been repeated so often that it is commonly accepted as gospel and is frequently cited, erroneously, to explain the fact that Erica and Alicia both have serious medical problems.

Many residents of New Sweden are related to one another, if only by marriage, and most will gladly recite a verbal matrix of second cousins, aunts, and uncles so intricate that it is impossible for an outsider to follow.

Jerry Nelson described his own familial connections this way: "My dad and Ralph Ostlund were half brothers. Oscar's mother and my dad and Ralph were first cousins, so Oscar and I are second cousins. Erica's father is my second and third cousin. Erica's father, Carl's grandmother, and my grandmother were sisters. Carl and I are second cousins—Carl's father and my father were first cousins. On the other side, Carl's grandfather was first cousin to my grandmother.

"There's a saying in Swedish: If you're not relatives, you're relatives of relatives."

Among non-Swedes, said Marilyn Kerr, there is a less tasteful saying. "What do they do in New Sweden for Halloween? They pump kin."

Doug McIntire was among those who bought the myth about Carl and Lois being first cousins. "That didn't stop me from making bad jokes about inbreeding up there," he said. "Please, that place is a bad scene out of *Deliverance.* Everybody's like a weird banjo boy."

Erica Grace suffers from a brain and spinal disorder known as syringomyelia with the Arnold-Chiari malformation. It is not believed to run in families and can be caused by trauma to the spinal cord or congenital developmental problems.

With syringomyelia, a cyst forms within the spinal cord, eventually destroying the center of the cord. With the Arnold-Chiari malformation, the lower part of the cerebellum protrudes from the back of the head into the neck.

Erica believes this makes her an easy target for murder. "I don't have any skull to protect my brain," she said. "One tap to the back of my head, and I could die. People are aware of this. I don't know if Norma knows in detail how serious it is, but she knows I've been sick in the past."

Norma has never threatened Erica, nor has she ever been known to be violent; but Erica watches over her shoulder with vigilance, especially in church. "I sit in the back pew or upstairs in the balcony," she said. "I will not let this woman be behind me."

Grunt Work

About four months after the poisoning, in early September, Col. Michael Sperry, chief of the Maine State Police, told a Bangor television reporter that police were still convinced the poisoning was a conspiracy. He also said they had a suspect who was aware that he or she was under suspicion. He did not offer a name.

Sperry's remarks hit New Sweden like a missile. People began to anticipate an arrest any day. Editors and news directors made contingency plans to get crews to Aroostook County on short notice.

But several weeks went by, and nothing happened. Two months later, Sperry still insisted that the case would be solved.

"We've had people that were involved in a crime, and something happens, and they come forward, give this information; we solve the crime," Sperry explained, "like James Hicks, that serial killer from Bangor—remember him?"

Few Mainers don't remember James Hicks, who spent almost twenty years getting away with murder, until a relentless state police detective named Joe Zamboni brought him to justice. According to Sperry, Zamboni is one of Maine's sharpest investigators.

At fifty-two, Joe Zamboni considers himself a "grunt." After three years as a state trooper, he was promoted to detective, and that's where he stayed for twenty-two years. One of his more memorable cases involved a man whose father beat him nearly to death with an iron pipe over the son's sexual relationship with the family dog. Being a detective was interesting, if nothing else. Zamboni would have accepted a promotion, but ass kissing was not his strong suit, so a grunt he remained.

Zamboni was also the founder of the Emergency Response Team, Maine's answer to *CSI*, consisting of detectives, troopers, medical examiners, forensic anthropologists, and scientists who cover major crimes, including the New Sweden arsenic poisoning. As part of the ERT he helped to create, Zamboni spent several weeks in New Sweden investigating the arsenic poisoning and Danny Bondeson's death.

Zamboni believes he knows who poisoned the church coffee and why. He also believes that to solve any crime, you must develop a rapport with the suspect. To prove that, he recounted the story of James Hicks, a case so macabre it could have come straight from Alfred Hitchcock:

"Jimmy Hicks married Jennie in high school. They were married several years, had two children, and she was getting ready to leave him. And she disappeared one day, and her family knew something had happened to her, because she was a young mother with two children, and she would not just disappear; she wouldn't abandon her children. It was reported to the Sheriff's Department, and a deputy came out, and he interviewed a couple of people in the trailer park, and Jimmy said she ran off with a truck driver. Deputy says, 'Okay, case closed,' which is kind of sad. Then the family went to the state police. And the state police said, 'Well, gee, this is the Sheriff's Department's case; we don't want to step on their toes. It's a missing persons case. We're not going to do anything, either.' The family was stunned.

"Six years later a woman disappears out of a bar in Newport. The bartender says, 'Yeah, there's a guy that comes in here, his name is Hicks. I'm not sure his name is Hicks, but I'm pretty sure they were drinking together.' So the patrolman goes and talks to Hicks. 'Were you drinking in a bar a couple of weeks ago with this woman?' Hicks says, 'Oh, I drink with women there all the time. It's possible, I don't know. What's her name?' The patrolman says, 'I know all about you. I know your wife disappeared six years ago. And that was pretty bizarre.'

"When he said that—he's a kind of an in-your-face kind of guy anyway—Jimmy started choking. 'I need water.' So he gets a glass of water. He's shaking. At that moment, his significant other walks through the door. She looks at the cop and says, 'What are you doing in my house?' 'Just asking Jimmy a few questions.' She says, 'I think this discussion is over. You can leave now. Get out of my house.' That was the last time Jimmy talked to the cops; that was 1982.

"Newport police went to the state police and said, 'We've got a problem here. We've got two missing women.' So the state police opened up an investigation in 1982. And they didn't do anything about the woman who disappeared from the bar. But on the wife's case—Jennie—this is too much: There was no report, no paperwork. The Sheriff's Department says they did all the reports, they gave them to the state police, and the state police lost them. State police said, 'They never gave us any reports.' So, which side do you believe?

"They found out that Jimmy had a friend who picked up this girl hitchhiking, a fifteen-year-old girl, and brought her home, was having sex with her. Then he dropped her off with Jimmy. He said, 'She's a runaway from Massachusetts. You can either baby-sit her, or she can live here with you.'

"She was there a few weeks, maybe a couple of months. So state police found her in Massachusetts; she's several years older. She says, 'Oh, yeah, I remember that night. I'd been out with the guy who picked me up hitchhiking. He dropped me off, we'd had a few beers; it was, like, one in the morning. I walked in the trailer, and Jimmy was sitting there with a beer, and the TV was on, but the stations had gone off the air; it was static, and Jennie was lying on the couch, but her head was in a funny position; it didn't look quite right to me. I said, 'Hi, Jimmy,' and went in the bedroom. When I woke up in the morning, it's ten o'clock and Jennie's not there; I didn't think much of it. The kids were staying with their grandparents. And Jimmy comes home at four or five and says, 'Where the hell's Jennie?' I said, 'She wasn't here when I got up.' He says, 'That's not right. I'm gonna call the cops.' I was scared to death. So I left, and I was too scared to tell anybody what happened. I left.'

"Okay, so Jennie's family tells the cops, look, her pocketbook and her glasses were there that morning. She wouldn't leave without her pocketbook and glasses. She can't see without her glasses. Do we have her pocketbook and glasses? No. Do we have a police report that says her pocketbook and glasses were there? No. We have nothing. We have absolutely nothing. So they take this case to court. They charged him with murder, and they took it to court. And it was all hearsay evidence. The family came in and said she wouldn't leave, we haven't heard from her in seven years. And the jury came back with a fourth-degree homicide conviction. That's under the old criminal code, the equivalent of manslaughter. The judge gave the maximum, ten years.

"So Jimmy got ten years, served six, which is standard. And he got released from prison in 1991; so now he's back out. In 1995, I'm in the office, get a call from the Brewer police: 'There's a guy here filing a complaint he's being harassed. His name's Jimmy Hicks. He's that guy who killed his wife, got convicted of murder, never found the body.' I said, 'Okay, I'll come over and talk to him.'

"I say, 'Jimmy, what's going on?' He says, 'This guy's going around taking video pictures of me, and I want it to stop. He thinks I killed his sister, Jerilyn Towers. She disappeared from a bar in Newport, like ten years ago, and he thinks I did it.' 'Well, why does he think you did it?' 'I don't know why he thinks I did it.' 'Well, I'll go talk to him.'

"So I go to Vance Taylor, who has done ten years in the state prison for shooting at the police. This guy is like a mountain. He tells me he's been doing his own investigation, and he's convinced that Jimmy killed his sister. I said, 'We'll work together, all right?' I went back to Jimmy and I said, 'Jimmy, this guy's nobody to screw around with. He's gonna kill you.' Jimmy says, 'I ain't afraid of him.' So I said, 'Look, Jimmy, I can help you out here. I can help you out. We get you cleared out of the Jerilyn Towers case; Vance will be off your back.' Jimmy says, 'Yeah okay, all right.'

"So that's how we developed our relationship. I was going to help Jimmy get out of this. First thing I wanted was a polygraph test. I said a polygraph test will take care of it. 'Oh, yeah, I want to take a polygraph test,' he says. But he never would—just lied to me.

"So we did this back and forth, and he's got this girl-friend living with him, Lynn Willette. So, we'd be talking, and he'd say, 'Anytime I talk to you, I want it recorded.' I said no problem. 'Not only that, I want a witness. I want Lynn sitting here while I talk to you.' No problem. So, we'd have these conversations. We'd talk about the Jennie Hicks case. And I'd say, 'Jimmy, you did your time for Jen. It's not an issue anymore. Don't care about that. We've got to get you out from under this Jerilyn Towers thing.' I said, 'Lynn, don't you think it would make sense for him to take a poly—' 'Nah,' she says. 'He's a big boy, he can make his own decisions.'

"So this went on for, like, four, five months. Guess what. I get a call from Brewer—Lynn Willette's disappeared. Jimmy came in to report her missing. This is the third time. I'm thinking, what am I gonna do? So we're like all over him, you know? Now, I know his personality. I know if you get in his face, and if you say 'Jimmy, goddammit, I know that you killed Lynn,' that's it. You're done talking. Okay?

Can't do that. That's the last thing I would do. So I said, 'Jimmy, what do you think happened?' He said, 'She was despondent—I'll bet she killed herself.' So I say, 'Okay, let's find her. Let's work together and find her.'

"It's like a moth and a flame. He thinks he's smarter than I am, and this is fun. It would stress him, and at the same time he couldn't resist. It was like some kind of game with him. So we developed this relationship, and I just popped in on him anytime.

"We found Lynn's car a few weeks later at a truck stop. Two o'clock in the morning I go knocking on his door. He comes to the door. I said, 'Good news—I found Lynn's car.' He says, 'What was in it?' I said, 'Nothing.' 'Really?' he says. And I go, 'Don't you worry, Jimmy.'

"I go see him a couple of weeks later. He says, 'What did you find in the car?' 'Nothing, Jimmy. There was nothing in the car.' 'That's bullshit.' I say, 'No, no.' He says, 'I'll tell you what's in the car. Under the seat there's receipts from Texaco. There's a little calendar book; there's a little pendant; she had this butterfly thing on the mirror . . .'

"He named twelve separate items that were in the car. Jimmy Hicks never drove Lynn's car. He had his own car; she had her own car. If they ever went anywhere together— macho man—she had to ride with him in his car. He's sitting there rattling off everything that was in this car. That's typical of what he would do. Obviously, he shouldn't say anything. But now he's telling me he's been all over her car, right? He knows exactly what's in that car, and when I tell him there's nothing in that car, he tells me what's in the car, what we found on our search. That's how it went for, like, years, back and forth, back and forth.

"This is like friendly coercion, you know? I learned this a long time ago. If you get in somebody's face and you act like a jerk, it's very easy for them to say 'I don't want to talk to you anymore.' If you're nice to them, you put them in a really awkward position. It's hard for them to kick you out. He had three wives. He had, the last I knew, seventeen illegitimate children. He had three or four wives; he always had a live-in girlfriend. He had one girl he kept in a little camper in his mother's backyard with a baby. That's how bizarre this guy is.

"So his latest girlfriend, we got female cops to pick her up off the street and try to talk to her. She filed a complaint with the DA's office saying I was harassing her and that I was 'harassing Mr. Hicks.' He wouldn't come to me and say, 'You asshole, stay away from me.' He'd send her, right? So they left the state. Human Services kept taking their kids; she kept having kids; Human Services kept taking them. So they went to where she'd lived down in Texas. So I was talking to one of his ex-wives, and she was a character. She's about this tall, and about this wide, she's got tattoos all over her, swears like a friggin' pirate. She said Jimmy had called from Texas and told her I'd been down there following him around. I said, 'I wasn't down in Texas following him around.' She starts laughing and says, 'I know, but I told him you were.'

"That really freaked him out. Basically, he flipped. He was working for this woman, doing some painting in her house. His girlfriend and he are in the van, and they pull in. And he's drinking, and he walks into the house in the middle of the afternoon and puts a beer down on the table. She's a fundamentalist lady in a nice neighborhood, and she says, 'What are you doing?' He grabs the phone, yanks the wire out, closes the blinds, pulls out a gun—it's actually a pellet gun, but she doesn't know that—puts it to her head and says, 'Write what I tell you to write.' He has her write a note saying she's despondent and she's going to leave her car to Jimmy Hicks. Then he goes in the bathroom and he fills the tub with water. He made some concoction out of Tylenol 3 and some other shit and made her drink it. He's like, right out of it. He's acting like an absolute freak. I mean, his girlfriend is sitting out in the driveway; it's the middle of the afternoon.

"So he asks the lady if she's got any guns. She says, 'My late husband had some guns in the closet.' And he says, 'Where?' and she says, 'Over there.' So he goes over there, and she goes out the front door. She ran out the door and ran to the neighbor's house, and told them to call the police. So the neighbor's son gets in the van, follows Jimmy while they're calling the police. And Jimmy goes to a couple of Dumpsters; he's throwing stuff in the Dumpsters. So meantime the cops are looking for him; they find him; they arrest him, and then the son takes the cops to all the Dumpsters, and they found the note that he had ripped up; they found the gun, you know, they found all the evidence.

"So I get a call. See, I'd been down there; I'd been working with these guys. So I get a call, 'You're not gonna believe what this nut did.' I said, 'Really?' So I go out and see Jimmy's brother, because I worked with the family. And he says, 'Jimmy's been calling me every day collect from the jail. He's driving me crazy.' I said, 'Well, what's he saying?' 'Well, he hates it down there; he says it's a Texas jail, and there's a bunch of Hispanics, and he does not get along with Hiss-panics.' I said, 'Really? Well, when he calls tomorrow, you tell him I'll cut him a deal with the AG's office, get him out of there and get him up here. Of course, he's gonna have to cooperate with me. But I can help him out.' 'Okay, I'll tell him.' Next day, or two days later, I get a call: 'Hicks wants to talk to you and the AG. He wants to make a deal.'

"It took me almost four months to get that worked out. So Jimmy said he wouldn't tell me what I wanted to hear until he got out of Texas. He says, 'I don't trust anybody.' And I said, 'Well, you gotta tell me something.'

"I flew down to Texas, and I said, 'You're gonna have to give me something. You've got to give me something.' He says, 'Oh, okay. I admit I killed Lynn Willette.' I said, 'Good. Tell me how.' He goes, 'Aw, Jesus, I don't really want to. Let's just say it wasn't an accident, okay?' He told me a couple of little things. I said, 'Okay, close enough.' I got the warrant. Got the extradition thing done.

"Let's see, how did he kill her? I think he strangled her. He dismembers all of them. I'm on the plane. I've got him in shackles, right? We're coming back. He's never told anybody anything. And he told me he killed Lynn Willette, and that's the only thing he's ever told anybody. He's sitting there beside me; we're eating, you know those croissants on the airplane? And it's like this: He says, 'You want those, uh, chips?' I say, 'You want my chips? You can have the chips.' 'Thanks,' he says, 'So anyway, I went to Shaw's, and I got one of them serrated knives, you know, about this long?' I said, 'Yeah?' He says, 'Her arms came off easy, but I had a hell of a time getting her head off.' I said, 'Really?' He says, 'How about the pickle? You want the pickle?' 'No, you can have the pickle.' 'Oh, thanks. So, anyway, I cut them off, and I put them in a bucket, and I mixed up some cement,' and blah blah blah . . .

"So this is like an hour and a half conversation on the airplane coming back. He's just spilling all of this detail out. Now when I go into the case, defense attorneys and private investigators who have worked these cases over the years told me that Jennie was in cement. They said, 'We'll deny that we ever told you. But the information we got, she's in cement.' And we'd always look for her, in cement steps, cement slabs. That's all they would tell me. That's it: 'She's in cement. That's all we know.' So we were always looking for cement, right? So, you know what he did?

"This is what happened: He killed Jennie. He cut off her head, and he put her head in a Coleman cooler, and filled the cooler with cement. He then put the Coleman cooler out on his deck. Jennie's father came by and said, 'Jimmy, what in God's name did you fill a brand-new Coleman cooler with cement for?' He said, 'Well, I need ballasts. I'm building a tower, a radio tower. I gotta have some weight.' Of course, he got scared, and he went out and buried it in the backyard. Jimmy told us, 'Dig under this tree.' We dig under the tree, and we find a cement block the size of a cooler—*boom*, broke it open—skull. Years earlier, her father had been standing right next to that Coleman cooler on the deck—not knowing his daughter's head was inside."

As part of the deal brokered by Zamboni, Hicks also confessed to killing Jerilyn Towers. Police found her body buried in his backyard.

"The whole key to that case was being able to get him to talk," Zamboni said. "I had to have a rapport with him to get him to talk to me. Since we had no crime scene, since we had no evidence whatsoever, the only hope we had of getting anything had to come from him. He was the only source, so it was absolutely essential to build a relationship."

In the case of the arsenic poisoning, the failure of investigators to maintain a relationship with the Bondesons was a major source of frustration to Bill Stokes. By making their suspicions known, the police effectively severed their connection to their primary sources of information—Norma and Carl Bondeson, both of whom were cooperative at the beginning.

"I would like to know more about Danny Bondeson," Stokes said. "The obvious place to go for that information would be the family. It would be nice to be able to talk to them."

"This is a very close-knit area," observed Jerry Nelson. "You want people to clam up, you do exactly what state police did. They tried to scare them. This may work in some places, but it surely won't work with a bunch of Swedes. It makes them stubborn."

At the beginning, Norma agreed to repeated interviews with police, gave her fingerprints and DNA, and even submitted urine samples to be tested for arsenic levels, which, incidentally, were normal. She did not hire an attorney. She also took a polygraph examination, but the results were inconclusive. Zamboni offered an explanation for this.

"A polygraph measures reaction," he said. "If your husband gets murdered, and you're a suspect, and somebody says, 'Did you kill your husband?' and you didn't, you know what's going on in your head? You're thinking, 'I was really a bitch to him, I really am sorry I did that. I didn't kill him, but now I feel bad because of the things I did to him'—it's going to get a reaction. A skilled polygraph operator is going to be able to see through that and ask all the questions that clarify. I'll give you a good example: I had a case one time where a deputy sheriff was sexually abusing his thirteen-year-old neighbor. I got a confession out of him. Then I realized he had to take a polygraph to get his job. How did he pass his polygraph? So I went to the polygraph operator, and I said, 'Let's go through this test again.' What happened was, the polygraph operator asked this question: Have you done anything that you are ashamed of? And he said, 'Yes I have.' Polygraph operator said, 'Well, what did you do?' And he said, 'I was unfaithful to my wife; I cheated on my wife.' The polygraph guy says, 'Have you done anything else?' The guy says, 'No, just being sexually unfaithful to my wife.' They go on to the next question. So the polygraph operator was not skilled enough to explore that.

"The rule of thumb on a polygraph is that you can't use a polygraph in court. So if a person fails it, and they give you a confession as a result of the polygraph, that's good. Say I give you a polygraph, and you fail it. I say, 'You failed it—obviously you're lying.' And you go, 'Okay, you got me—I did it.' That's it. I've got a confession. That's valuable. If you fail the test, and I say, 'You flunked the test—you're lying to me,' and you say, 'Screw you,' what have I got? I've got that you flunked the test. What does it mean? It doesn't really mean that much, because there are so many things that could explain it. The only thing that counts is when they confess afterwards. That's what counts. Or if they pass it. If they pass it solidly, that makes you feel better.

"See, I think what confused the police a little bit is that Norma is probably displaying this guilt—it was her brother. And if I am correct, she would come home and say, 'Know what those bastards said about me today?' Now she sees what Danny did, and she's going to feel guilty. So if you read the guilt as culpability instead of what normal people would feel, you can get confused.

"What I am saying is that it's quite possible that she is feeling tremendous guilt. It's her brother. They probably had conversations about the church, and she could have even said, 'God knows I'd like to kill those people,' innocently. And now it's like, oh, my God. She probably feels in some way she did make him do it. How could she not?"

Cracking Nuts and Eating Sweets

On a snowy Saturday in February 2004, a reporter was invited to the home of Herman and Karla Fisher. Lois Anderson had come with her daughter Erica Grace, who had organized the gathering, and all five sat down at the dining room table to talk. Herman and Karla had agreed to speak to the writer at Erica's urging; they said it was because they wanted to get the truth out about the arsenic poisoning—not only the incident itself, but the problems that may have led up to it. Until now, ten months after the poisoning, they had not been ready to talk.

The reporter had endured many months of silence and repeated rejection by almost all of the arsenic survivors, but this day was different. To her surprise, she was served delicious cups of hot coffee, a lovely assortment of Swedish pastries, and a river of slurs about Norma Bondeson.

"I'm not scared of her, but there are a lot of people who are," Herman said. "We know she's so friggin' involved in this, but we don't know exactly what she did. We're doing our best to get rid of her, and we're trying to be as tactful as we can."

"If she masterminded the whole thing, it wouldn't surprise me," Karla added. "She's directly or indirectly involved. Whenever she comes into the room, everybody tenses up. One day at church, she started to go out in the kitchen, and it wasn't two seconds when Erica got out of her seat and was right behind her."

Erica guffawed, pounding the table. "Oh yeah, I remember that!"

Herman folded his hands and leaned toward the writer.

"We watch her very closely," he said. "We tolerate her, but she doesn't make a move. It's going to be hard to break her. It's going to be tough; she's a tough nut to crack."

The writer was puzzled. Has anyone simply asked Norma if she was involved in the poisoning, or asked her what she knows?

"Oh, she says she didn't do anything; she doesn't know anything." Erica's voice was singsong. "She doesn't know why people treat her the way they do. She says the military is nasty to her because she never retired. She said she had to get done because she was older. She told a lot of people that. They forced her out—they made her get done. She does this whole sympathy act, oh, yeah!"

Erica was at least partly right. Norma's retirement was originally scheduled for 1993, and she challenged it, applying to the Air Force for a waiver. Her commander, Col. Robert J. Winner, stood firmly behind her. In a memorandum dated January 22, 1993, Winner praised Norma as "a valuable, trained asset" during the Gulf War, flying injured soldiers from Saudi Arabia to military hospitals in Europe. "She has consistently contributed to the excellence of her unit," he wrote.

By all accounts, Norma's career was impressive. After graduating from Caribou High School in 1959, she attended Clara Maass Memorial Hospital in Belleville, New Jersey, and became a registered nurse before enlisting in the Air Force. During almost twenty-seven years of service, she spent twenty of them as a flight nurse, accumulating more than two thousand hours in the air. She received a chief flight nurse badge, completed Squadron Officers' School, Air Command and Staff College, and the Air War College. In the 1990s, she was deployed during Operation Desert Shield and Desert Storm, and "performed her duties in an exceptional manner," according to another commander, Col. Carl A. Merwin. He added that she was a "highly motivated professional" whose "contributions to quality training and unit morale are exceptional and consistent."

Norma's wish for a waiver was granted, but only temporarily. In 1996, at age fifty-five, she was transferred to retired-reserve status. On June 14, 2001, her sixtieth birthday, and Flag Day on the American calendar, she began collecting her pension.

Despite Norma's impeccable service record, both her career and her marital status were a source of suspicion to Herman.

"Here's a woman who's never been married," he said, "so she didn't have to learn to cooperate with a husband or anything, you know—the give and take. So she's used to having people doing as they're told. She's used to having her way. And every time you talk to her, she brings up military terms: 'Chain of command.' What the hell do these people care about chain of command? I understand where she's coming from, but nobody else does. She liked to talk to me because she knew I was military. The military was probably the biggest and best thing that ever happened to her."

After the poisoning, Norma could scarcely make a move that did not rankle those who disliked her. About three months after the poisoning, she brought to church a vase containing lovely white flowers with orange centers, and set them down near the altar. They were blossoms from the last crop of potatoes planted by her brother Danny.

"Norma comes waltzing her charming little ass right down past me, right past the organ," Karla said. "And she's got this little pitcher; it's about this tall, about that big around, with friggin' potato blossoms in it. Now, she would've known that would bother everybody a lot."

"As a matter of fact," Herman added, "they couldn't even be seen where she put them."

"But she came in late," said Karla, "so everybody could see her."

Some tried to defend Norma.

"Janet and Shirley stood up for her about the damn potato blossoms," Karla said. "They said, 'Well, she brought those in memory of Danny.' I'm like, 'Bullshit. She came and brought those just to rub it in my face.'"

The Fishers admit they have no evidence that Norma had anything to do with the poisoning, but that does not dampen their belief that she was somehow responsible.

"It's possible that Norma didn't have anything to do physically with this," Herman said. "But she knew; I will swear that she knew what was going to happen, and she could have prevented it. Remember the comment she made: 'What I know I'll take to my grave.'"

It is significant that the Fishers are aware of this comment, which Norma reportedly made to investigators during one of her interviews. After the arsenic survivors were released from the hospital, they had regular meetings, a support group of sorts, which detectives would sometimes attend and share provocative bits and pieces of what Norma had told them. As a result, the survivors and their families learned to examine Norma's every word for double meanings and sinister messages.

"One day not too long ago," Erica said, reaching for a lemon pastry, "Norma was talking about going out with Sven to pick his potatoes, and how it was cold, and how Finn couldn't go somewhere because he was helping, too. She said, 'You know how it is. You'll do whatever you have to do to protect your family, and to help your family out at whatever cost.' She said that to me."

Increasingly, Norma's seemingly innocent comments were endowed with nefarious meanings. Thoughtlessness was interpreted as depraved indifference. Karla described a misunderstanding that occurred when Norma mistakenly set up the communion table during a week when there would be no communion.

"I called her and said, 'Norma, we don't have communion this week because it's Palm Sunday next week.'

"She says, 'Well, I have to go set up communion when I have time, and today was the only day I had time.' And I said, 'I just thought I'd call and let you know. I'm taking care of my grandson. When he goes home, I'll try to run up and put it away for you.' She says, 'You're not doing it for me. You're doing it for *Gustaf Adolph Lutheran Church.*' And I said, 'What the hell ever.'"

Pouring Herman a cup of coffee, Karla continued.

"That was Wednesday. Friday night Norma calls to talk to Herman, and I answered the phone. 'Karla, while I've got you on the phone I should probably tell you I was a little short with you.' I said, 'Yes, you were.' She said, 'Well, I thought I should probably just tell you I had so many things going on that day, and I just wasn't thinking.' But she never said she was sorry. She doesn't care about people—about anyone."

As Karla's train gathered steam, Herman jumped on board.

"I get the impression—and I think I'm a fairly decent reader of people—that she is unemotional," he said. "First off, poisoning is a woman's weapon, right? We all know that. I think she would have no problem at all poisoning somebody. Danny may have been the one who put the stuff in the coffeepot, and he may not have. But I think he knew something, and he couldn't live with it."

"I think he knew and couldn't live with it," Lois agreed.

"I don't think it was remorse on his part," said Herman. "I think he found out that one member of his family poisoned us. I don't think Danny would dream this up by himself and do it."

"He was too compassionate," Lois said. "To teach children, and to work in a nursing home, you have to be compassionate. And he cared for his father."

Myra Burkhalter

Right after he left Gustaf Adolph, the Reverend Scottie Burkhalter began serving as pastor of St. Paul Lutheran Church in Maryville, Tennessee. The reverend was unwilling to speak to reporters, but during a phone call in the spring of 2004, his wife, Myra, was friendly and warm. She was also very cautious about what she said.

"It's nice here. We have a new church building. We average two hundred people a Sunday—two services. We're back where we're from; we're four hours from all of our family.

"Danny, he was always so helpful, wanting to do things. He was very giving, and anything you needed, he would be there. Our two cats came from his farm. The first one we got, that was Callie, she just died not too long ago. I think she got into some antifreeze somewhere at the neighbor's. We still have Smoky.

"Norma was real nice. Once the kids got started at Camp Calumet, boy, she and Carl and Kristine and the Blanchettes, they went wild over Calumet. It was just a nice place to take your kids; you can leave them there. It was a nice environment. We were very connected with the people there."

Did Fran yell at Scottie in the parsonage?

"No comment. Scottie's been real careful, and I don't want to do anything that's going to harm them or ourselves, especially with his career."

Did Julie yell at him after Barb Margeson's funeral?

"That I don't know."

Did you and Scottie really leave Gustaf Adolph just to be closer to your families?

Myra hesitated before answering.

"I guess. I mean, we just wanted to go where God called us."

Erica's Prayer

A frosty breeze nipped at Erica's cheeks as her boots crunched across the icy church parking lot. It was Friday, February 6, 2004, and as the new co-superintendent, she needed her materials to prepare for Sunday school. She held up her ring of keys, singled one out, and unlocked the back door. Instead of making her usual beeline to Svea Hall, she tiptoed into the sanctuary and glanced around. There was no sound except the whooshing and whistling of the wind outside. She sat down in a pew and took off her scarf and gloves. *This feels weird*, she thought, *I've never sat here by myself before and thought about religion and stuff. God help me nobody walks in here, because they're going to think that I've flipped the lid.*

She gazed at the wall behind the altar, where a large mural depicted Jesus kneeling in the Garden of Gethsemane. *That's kind of ironic*, she thought. Gethsemane is where, on the eve of his crucifixion, Jesus begged the Father to spare him from the poison of human sin: "O my Father, if it be possible, let this cup pass from me . . . if this cup may not pass away from me, except I drink it, thy will be done" (Matthew 26:39–42).

Erica closed her eyes and started to pray. God, I'm just asking, am I doing right—and in my heart I believe I'm doing right—by going after Norma and trying to find the truth? Whether she's involved or not, I need to know the truth for these people. Not to get over it, as everybody says, but to get through it. We need the truth to get through it. We're never going to get over it; I don't care who says it or what, we're not getting over this because I look at Herman, I look at my mother, and I look at Uncle Dale. I see them every day and what they go through. I'm not going to get over it, because they're not the same people they were before April 27. They are different people. They have been through hell and back.

Give me a sign, God, that I'm doing the right thing by trying to get this woman to crack, by trying to find the truth.

I just got chills and goose bumps. There's a sign.

God, is it wrong for me not to just forgive this woman and move on?

Erica stopped and waited.

She didn't get a chill, not even a little. *Okay*, she thought, *there's something there.* My angel is Reid Morrill, and Reid Morrill is going to put me in the right direction, isn't he, God? As close as Reid and I were, he's going to put me in the right direction. I believe he will. Mr. Reid is right there, saying, "Erica, you're doing the right thing. Keep doing it." And I honestly believe that; I do, wholeheartedly, that Reid Morrill is my angel, and he is going to help me get the strength to do this, and I have the strength to do it.

I'll make this woman go down; I'll make her crack, and I don't care. I may not be there the moment she cracks, but I've built her up to it. I've started to irritate the hell right out of her to no end.

But, God, I'm not doing anything that isn't right.

Erica stood up, filled with a new resolve to forge ahead.

She was more convinced than ever that she had been given a mission from God. "I've got to just figure out the perfect bomb to throw her, and do it," she said a few days later. "I'll throw one dig, and the next week, throw another dig. I'll get her; I will. I have full faith that I will, and the truth will be known."

Someone Who's Not Going
to Take Their Crap

Several investigators on the arsenic poisoning case were convinced from the very beginning that Norma was behind the crime. This belief was based largely on the premise that the church was divided between "traditionalists" and "contemporaries," and that Norma was a diehard traditionalist. "She (poisoned the coffee) to teach them not to defy the traditional teachings of the Lutheran Church," one investigator theorized.

The problem with this theory was that the underlying premise was false—Norma was not a traditionalist. In fact, she was a staunch advocate for change.

"Norma is a very passionate person in the church," said Doug McIntire, whom, incidentally, the police have never interviewed. "I was her buddy when I was there; I liked her. I liked that she wanted the church to be more faith based. She wasn't interested in maintaining the status quo. She wanted Camp Calumet pushed. She wanted us to find the money somewhere to send every kid within or even outside the church to go to Calumet. She was able to step outside herself from within the church, and look around and say,

'Whoa, there's a lot of old people here.' She wanted the kids to be brought up in the faith. She wanted the children to be brought up in the church and not to lose interest and go away. At one point we were trying to get contemporary services off the ground. A lot of people my age were going to try and work in a contemporary service midweek. Norma was in favor of that.

"Norma wanted to fill the church. It was a genuine desire to bring people in. When I was on the council, she'd talk my ear off about all this, hoping I'd be a catalyst for change since I was the young outsider moving in. So she was really hoping that I would help institute these changes when I left the council, and shortly before I left, she was put on the council; she took my place. And I think she started to realize that she was beating her head against the wall with some of these people. There was a little more frustration in her voice when we would talk about such things as Christian education, and bringing people in, and Camp Calumet.

"The worst blow was when Scottie was trying to get more funding for Calumet, and they shut him down. A lot of it was around the children, educating the children around the church. She couldn't get over the Calumet situation. The synod was ready to offer money—I believe it was matching funds—they were going to offer us all the money to set up our own camp if we would just put in a little bit of money and the footwork and do it. And that was what the council shot down; that was Scottie's last straw, and that blew Norma away. The council wasn't willing to offer up the pocket change."

Norma did not let the council's decision stand between the children and Camp Calumet.

"Most of the kids can go there for practically free," said Sally Sandstrom, "because she comes around all summer and collects bottles, and she saves all the money for Camp Calumet. That's her nature of giving."

"I think Norma has a healthy faith," Doug said. "She may not always be right, but she believes it and tries to live it. She was very direct, zealous, energetic, and very animated when she would speak. She would get very worked up, very emotional. I've heard her stand up and address the Calumet situation: 'We have to take care of the kids; we have to see to the kids' needs and do whatever it takes to see that that happens.' And when she would talk to me personally about all these things, she would be very emphatic about how we need to change. The council was keeping the status quo, and they were ineffective.

"The Ruggles and the Fishers were interested in just keeping the ball rolling, the status quo, what they'd been doing for years and years. Many times it would come down to the people on Worship and Music. Norma would come up to me all the time, 'Why aren't you up there preaching more often?' I'd say, 'Go talk to Worship and Music, they're the ones that make the schedule.' She'd say, 'Well, maybe I will. This is ridiculous; you're going to seminary. I'd like to see you up there every Sunday.'

"She would say to me, 'What we really need is a good old-fashioned Missouri Synod pastor to come in here and straighten these people out, someone who's not going to take their crap.'"

Doug laughed. "That was her big line—someone who would come in, put his foot down, put all the children in their seats, tell them what their place is and what his place is, and take charge. Scottie was on the edge of doing that, but he didn't have the experience, and they ran him out of town.

"She was not confrontational; she liked to keep a safety zone. She knew she was safe talking to me and airing things to me.

"Norma got angry and frustrated. Exasperated would be the best term. She would just get very tightly wound over things; for the most part, though, she was easygoing. It was always about the church. I never knew she had a boyfriend. Just the church. I think she once mentioned she was a nurse, and the Air Force, and that was it. It was all about the church. She would always stay late and help put things away, help clean up after the coffee. She was very helpful. She'd lend a hand wherever she could."

Doug finds the suggestion that Norma would put arsenic in the church coffee ludicrous. "Norma's a nurse, and she would find something better than a fistful of arsenic," he said. "Think about it. She's bright. She's too bright to say, 'Danny, you're going to take some arsenic and throw it in the coffeepot.'

"It wasn't a bright crime. A nurse would come up with something better than throwing some arsenic in the coffee. And especially if it was just to make them sick and not to kill them. You don't use arsenic to make people ill; you use arsenic to kill people. I give her far more credit than that. But Danny—think about it—he was a farmer; he grew up in that community where they used this as a top killer, and there's probably some country legend of 'so and so got some mixed up, and oh boy, didn't he get sick.' You hear those things all the time—'So and so froze his thumb off.' Stupid little stories. So you have someone like Danny, not thinking of it as arsenic but as 'that's what made so and so sick.'

"I think what may have happened is Norma was suddenly chewing Danny's ear off about the whole deal: 'This needs to change; if only those people didn't show up,' and so forth. There were times when I was there after the service, and she talked about reforming the church for a couple of hours, easy. It may be that Danny thought, 'I'll make my sister feel better. I was doing the right thing.' And he goes off the deep end. To me that makes about as much sense as anything else that's come out of this, because really, she can go on and on. And if she did it to me at the church, God knows what she does at home."

Posthumous Privilege

In the days immediately following the poisoning, Daniel Bondeson had two consultations with a criminal defense lawyer in Caribou. What Danny told attorney Peter Kelley during those meetings has become like the Holy Grail to investigators, and Stokes has been doggedly pursuing it since Danny died. Kelley has refused to disclose what he knows, citing privilege, which remains in force even after a client's death. He has said he will be happy to share the information only if he receives an unconditional waiver of privilege from Daniel's estate. "If people are injured, I guess they can sue," he said. "I don't think it's very likely, but if whatever I said implicated him in any way, it may expose the estate to lawsuits, and if so, would be due to my breaching the confidential relationship I had with Danny."

Kelley had several negotiating sessions with Alan Harding, a Presque Isle attorney who represents Daniel Bondeson's estate, and Harding offered a partial waiver, which would allow Kelley to speak only to authorities and to Harding himself. Kelley said "No dice" to this arrangement, explaining he did not want his words to be filtered through anyone else. "If the waiver is granted, then I want to be free to talk to anybody," he said, "and I can't seem to get that."

More than a year after the poisoning, Bill Stokes was still looking for ways to compel Kelley to reveal what he knows. Stokes was also keeping his eye on a case in North Carolina that has eerie similarities to this one, the death of a thirty-year-old AIDS researcher named Eric Miller.

On November 15, 2000, Eric Miller went bowling with his wife, Ann, and some friends. Eric had a beer and a hot dog and then became violently ill. The next day his wife took him to the hospital. After a week, his condition dramatically improved, and he went home. A week later, he became sick again, was taken to the hospital, and died. By then, doctors had discovered arsenic in his blood.

Police decided he was murdered and found telephone records of calls between Eric's wife, a researcher at a drug company, and her coworker Derril Willard. Police said they were having an affair, and that it had been Willard who handed Eric the beer at the bowling alley just before he got sick. They also discovered that Ann Miller had telephoned Willard after midnight on the night her husband had died.

The medical examiner determined that arsenic had been administered to Eric several times over a period of months. Police searched the lab where Ann Miller and Derril Willard worked and found that arsenic was among the chemicals to which they had access.

Ann Miller denied being involved in her husband's death, hired attorneys, and refused to talk further with the police.

After meeting once with detectives, Derril Willard consulted with an attorney, Richard Gammon. The next day, Willard committed suicide, leaving behind a note denying he killed Eric.

With the investigation now at a standstill, the conversation that Willard had with Gammon became a critical piece of evidence, and prosecutors asked the North Carolina

Supreme Court to force the attorney to reveal what Willard had told him.

The court ruled that a trial court judge had the authority to decide what portions of the conversations between Willard and Gammon were not covered by privilege, noting that Willard could have implicated a third party without incriminating himself, and that those portions of the conversation would not be privileged. Gammon turned a transcript of the conversation between him and his client over to a trial court judge, who selected twelve lines that reportedly implicated a third party.

On September 27, 2004, a grand jury in Raleigh, North Carolina, indicted Ann Miller on a charge of first-degree murder in connection with her husband's death, and that evening, she surrendered to authorities. As of this writing, she is being held without bail at the Wake County Jail, awaiting trial.

If the North Carolina ruling were applied to the New Sweden case, Peter Kelley would be required to turn over whatever portions of his conversations with Danny implicated a third party but did not incriminate Danny. Asked if the North Carolina ruling would be relevant in this case, Kelley responded, "Maybe."

Not surprisingly, Erica has dreamed up her own theory about why the Bondeson estate has not granted Kelley the waiver of privilege. "You see, Peter Kelley couldn't tell Carl and Norma what he knows; you've got to look at it that way," she said. "They don't know what Danny said, so it's, 'We've got to shut him right the hell up.' Carl and Norma are squirming. That's the way I look at it."

Zamboni's Theory

Joe Zamboni retired from the Maine State Police in early 2004. He only worked on the New Sweden arsenic poisoning for a relatively short time, but more than a year after the crime, he offered his theory on what probably happened.

"We don't know if Daniel Bondeson did it or not for sure. We don't know exactly what happened," he said. "But we know what this guy was like. To me, he fits the same kind of a profile as a guy who walks into a school and shoots the kids.

"He was a nice guy, and very frustrated. I heard that he went to school to be a teacher. He couldn't get a job as a teacher, so he had to substitute. I heard that kids locked him in the locker room one time. Obviously, he had no control.

"He was really into the Swedish thing. His trips to Sweden; he was very much into that. That gave him, I am sure, a feeling of success. I saw newspaper clippings of the things he did. Part of what was going on at the church was the struggle between Swedish culture and heritage and teachings of the church. Remember, you're dealing with a personality who was having a little trouble with reality.

Somebody who's probably making a lot more of things, thinking this is a lot more serious than everybody else thinks it is. The letter from the bishop said, 'You guys need to get back on track; you are too concerned with this Swedish traditional stuff; we've got to get back to the Gospel.' So if Danny finds this whole Swedish heritage thing incredibly important, and the bishop of the church is saying it's not important, what you believe in here is not important, it's not what this church is about, it's pretty hard for him to take. And that would definitely affect him.

"You've got a split. There are two groups, and there are hard feelings. A reasonably normal person can figure out that that's no big deal; it's just personalities and stupid stuff. But for somebody who has some mental issues, it would be very significant. He wasn't living normally. When people are having trouble with reality, are depressed, have issues in their life they can't face, they tend to not deal with it. When you go into somebody's house and you see the stuff from their parents and their grandparents still there that nobody could make a decision to keep this or throw it away, that shows a mental state. That's a person who is not dealing very well with reality.

"I'll tell you why the police are pointing the finger at Norma, why they say it's a conspiracy. I've been doing this for years. Whenever we have a murder, and we go into some town, and we ask, 'Who could have done this?' the people in town think of who's the biggest asshole in town: 'It's got to be him—he is the only one who could do this.' Well, it's got nothing to do with that person. But now you start getting it from all sides. The rumors start.

"Let's think about Norma for a minute. She's ex-military, been out of town for years and years. She's a strong woman. She also has a long history there, but she's been away. So she comes back in, and she starts to take charge of things, which pisses off a lot of people. So there are some people that really like her, and some people that really strongly dislike her and call her all sorts of bad names. So when something bad happens in the church, who do you think they're going to blame? Whoever the mean, bad person in the church is. That's normal. That's what you'd expect to see.

"But it turns out, the evidence points toward Danny. He's well liked; he's a nice guy. People like Danny, and they say it can't be him; he's a nice guy. It's gotta be the mean, old Norma. That's what people do, it's normal. But the police should be filtering it out.

"Now, hindsight is always twenty-twenty. But you have this terrible incident, and you start to get information, and then all of a sudden, you have a suicide, where the guy basically says, 'I did it.' The smart thing to do, I think, is to say, 'Well, case closed. Now we'll follow up. There are going to be issues that come forward, and we will follow up. But as far as we're concerned, this is pretty much over.' Then you wouldn't have all this.

"You have this person who killed himself. You have a note where he gives some sort of an explanation. Look at his history and his personality, and it all fits. It fits, okay? Now beyond that, you have conspiracy theories, which shouldn't be dismissed out of hand. You should devote some time to them. But the conspiracy theories are the little piece, and the big piece is already done. But the press conferences made the conspiracy the big news.

"Danny's a likable guy. But think about a person who's just so abnormal to poison a congregation. These are incredibly unusual cases. When have we ever had one before? An attempted mass murder—that's what this is. I think if you put arsenic in somebody's drink, when you think about it, it's no different from taking a gun and shooting at a house hoping you won't hit anybody. So, first of all, it is very, very unusual. This is not normal. So you're dealing with a mental issue—somebody who is cowardly, somebody who wants revenge, somebody who wants a feeling of power—and he is going to lash out in an absolutely crazy way. It's just like the kid that goes into a high school with a gun and shoots a bunch of innocent kids because he's angry. He's repressed this anger; he feels like the whole school is against him, and he's going to take out as many of them as he can.

"Can you imagine locking a teacher in a locker room? That bothered him much more than it should have. It's like a normal person would go into a school and say, 'I can't seem to control these kids. I guess I should get a different job.' And other people look at it like, 'They're out to get me.'

"I think he was just angry with some people in the congregation. When you have a rift in church, you have Side A and Side B, and they probably said hurtful things to each other. And he's probably being protective of his sister. Now his sister is this big, strong woman, and they're probably saying stuff to her, and she's probably coming home and saying, 'You know what those people said today, those rotten s.o.b.'s.' And he's like, 'They can't do that to my sister.' He's getting enraged.

"The rift over the communion table would be very hurtful for him, make him very angry. Another person would go up and say, 'Look, this is important, and we need to do this.' But he just internalizes it, goes in the corner. 'Those people are out to get me. I can't stand it anymore.'

"He obviously was mental, and he acknowledges he did it. And he's got the capability and the time to do it and then go home.

"Here are two crime scenes. The church was done in the first couple of days. Second, we go through the house, look for evidence, see what was there. We found stuff that showed his mental state. We found arsenic. We confirmed that certainly the arsenic could have come from there. It was old stuff from years ago. They outlawed it about twenty years ago, I think. Typically, a farmer who has arsenic used it on crops, and the government says it's illegal, they're not going to dump it out; they're going to leave it in the barn. So most all of those old farms had arsenic.

"There was no evidence of a conspiracy at the farm. The most logical way to look at this is, why would somebody do this? What's the motive? And how crazy do you have to be to do that? Norma's not crazy. She's a normal person. It doesn't fit. It doesn't make sense.

"It's so easy to influence somebody, so easy. And see, this is what's going on here. The gossip starts; the rumors start. And now all of a sudden people are believing as gospel what they have heard, and it feeds itself. And a year later they're absolutely convinced this is what happened.

"Only a crazy person would do such a thing. She's not crazy."

Shortly after the poisoning, a source close to the Bondeson family explained what might have motivated Danny to poison the church coffee. "Certain people had taken the church and created dissension in the church—their actions had made him sick," the source said. "Pastor Scottie had been abused, mistreated, and forced out unfairly. It wasn't the contemporaries versus the traditionalists. It was an alliance of the passives versus the aggressives. Danny's perspective was these people had taken over. He felt these others were in control, and improperly so. It was unethical. The church was his anchor, too. When he killed himself, I think he was truly remorseful. The only thing that gave the conspiracy theory any drive is that police were at a loss how to investigate it."

Eleven Cents, Please

The June 2004 issue of *Down East*, a magazine about Maine, featured a story entitled "New Sweden a Year After the Horror" on its cover. The article, by Jeff Clark, was accompanied by breathtaking photographs of New Sweden; its potato fields, its Midsommarfest, its cemetery, and a magnificent rainbow arching over a shingled farmhouse. Next to the picture was the following caption: "A year after the media frenzy that followed the church poisoning, the community—from the outlying farms to the local cemetery—has settled into its old ways. Though no one has been indicted, everyone in town knows who was behind the crime."

This outrageous caption is a textbook case of sloppy journalism and an excellent illustration of how the suspicion, innuendo, and rumors surrounding Norma Bondeson came to be accepted as proof of her involvement in a ghastly crime. The caption presumes there was a conspiracy and that there is a perpetrator at large; the accompanying article advances that presumption while offering no evidence to support it.

"If you ask anyone in town who else was involved," an anonymous resident told *Down East*, "you'll hear the same name every time. But knowing who it is and proving it in a court of law are two different things."

Joe Zamboni has witnessed this scenario countless times before.

"In these communities, they think of somebody who is either the local bad person, or in this case, somebody who was on the other side of the fight," he said. "And they point fingers, and then the rumors start, and they get bigger with time, and pretty soon everybody's convinced. It's based on personalities, nothing more, just personalities."

"People point their fingers at Norma, and it's not right," said Sally Sandstrom. "The way the police presented it, they made it sound like she was involved. They say they have an undercover cop still around her. It's been very rough on her. I've seen people attack her, and I've said, 'I just want to go home and have a good stiff drink.' And she'd say, 'Yeah, I think I'm going to go home and have a nice glass of wine.' She's riding this out in her own way."

Some afternoons Norma can be found at Stan's, a ramshackle store on the shore of Madawaska Lake, where penny candy, insect repellent, and blaze-orange hats are on display next to sparsely stocked aisles of groceries in dusty jars and dented cans. Sweatshirts embroidered with moose and loons, heavy-duty flannel gloves, and knives and tools of various shapes fill the shelves leading to the back of the store, where a framed collection of small silver spoons hangs over a monolithic upright piano. Cracked vinyl booths and wooden tables and chairs are adjacent to a big window that frames a magnificent view of the lake. Locals wander in after a morning of cross-country skiing, or a summer afternoon of kayaking, serenely faithful that the lopsided, dilapidated old roof won't come crashing down on their fried eggs and bacon or grilled cheese and chips. They pick up a *Bangor Daily News* or *Aroostook County Republican* to find fodder for long hours of lazy chat about stupid politicians and how taxpayers always get burned. Jerry Nelson, a regular at Stan's, calls it "the intellectual center of Madawaska Lake" and jokes that Stan himself "has become a Swede."

At the counter up front, hungry customers gaze at the printed menu up on the wall or the hand-scrawled paper signs tacked near the register announcing the daily specials: Rice Pudding $1.50, Corn Chowder $1.25. They dictate their order to Stan, who painstakingly records item and price with a nubby pencil on a dog-eared white notepad. He carefully adds up the numbers, then draws a line and writes down the total before reading it aloud and accepting their money. He rings the drawer open on the big metal register, places bills in their slots and coins in their cubbies, closes the drawer, and hands back the change with a smile that hints of mischief but guarantees honesty. Then he goes into the kitchen to cook. Patrons are welcome to use the rotary phone, but if nature calls, better go outside, and good luck finding a place that's private, because the ragged old store is squeezed on a spit of land between the gravel road and the lake.

"The first time I went into Stan's, I was looking for some cabins," recalled Kay Nash, who lived on Madawaska Lake. "I went in, and Stan was standing there with his arms crossed. His armpits were stained. He has a beard down to there, and I didn't know if there was a bird's nest in there or not. He asked me if I wanted something to eat. I said, 'No, thank you.'"

With all of his charm and personal idiosyncrasies, however, Stan has one true claim to fame: his eleven-cent coffee, of which he serves two-hundred and eighty cups every day.

"I have to tell you I have had his coffee," said Marilyn Kerr. "My daughter's come up, and we went down on a Sunday morning. There was nobody there; they were all at church. So my daughter and I went down and had coffee, and she said, 'Mom, it's the best coffee I've ever had. Give me a dollar; I'm going to get another cup.' And I gave her a dime and a penny and she says, 'What's that?' And I said, 'That's what the coffee costs.' She couldn't get over it."

Stan's also serves as a local gossip exchange. "If I didn't know what I was doing, I'd stop in there and they would tell me," Marilyn joked.

Each January, the regulars at Stan's put on a "black-tie potluck supper," sporting T-shirts with iron-on images of bowties at the neck. Newcomers are looked upon warily and are expected to act friendly first and tell folks who they are. After that, they are welcomed with a smile, and soon the place becomes a habit and begins to feel like home.

"I have to go down there to vote," Marilyn said. "They have a blue tarp, and they wrap it around the last booth. And everybody stops and looks at you when you walk in, and you tell them who you are—of course they know who you are—and they say, 'Well, you just wait a minute now.' So you sit down and you wait. Then it's your turn, and you go behind it and you sit down, and mark your ballot and put it in the box. It's just a little shoebox. It's funny because everybody just stops and looks at you because you're not one of the regulars."

Norma is considered one of the regulars at Stan's, and since few of the others live in New Sweden, it provides a refuge from the backbiting at the church. Or so it would seem. Brenda Jepson of Stockholm, who after the poisoning became a self-appointed representative for the Swedish Colony, told *Down East*, "There are people who won't go into Stan's if a particular car is parked outside. I'm one of them."

Jerry Nelson is a few years younger than Norma and has known her all of his life. He is certain she had nothing to do with the poisoning.

"I can't picture Norma doing it," he said. "Norma's too damn open. When she has something on her mind, she says it and it's over. She doesn't dwell on it."

A few times, Jerry and Norma have discussed the poisoning. "Norma and I talked many times at Stan's," Jerry said. "We'd talk about it, and try to figure out why Danny did it."

They also tried to figure out how he did it. Although investigators found an opened jug of sodium arsenic on the Bondeson farm, the Bondesons were never known to have used the substance as a top killer. "Norma told me she couldn't understand where it came from," Jerry said, "because as kids growing up, they had to wait for the killing frost before old Harold would let them harvest."

In fact, the Bondesons were among the first growers in New Sweden to move in the direction of organic farming. Daniel's older brother Peter, whose farm was just down the road from the original family farm, was particularly worried about the use of toxins as top killers, fearing the chemicals would seep down into the potatoes themselves.

"I lived with Peter for two years after I got divorced," Jerry said. "Peter and I talked a lot about farming. This was 1986 or '87. Peter was afraid of all this chemical usage. He thought the way to go was organic. Peter would walk the fields, and it disturbed him when we had a blight infestation, that some farmers said, 'I spray every five days whether it needs it or not.'"

While living with Pete, Jerry worked as a substitute teacher. "I was teaching special education classes," he said. "I took one of Pete's pigs down to the school, and the kids had a ball with it. Norma gave me a little sweater for it.

"She was always active in helping older people. She stayed home a lot with her mother, and came home to be with her father when he needed it. Thorborg had pancreatic cancer. They went through hell. It bothered Harold terribly.

"She and Danny were very close. After he died, she said, 'Why, why, why?' She had tears in her eyes. They were very close.

"I remember a potluck supper at Stan's, and Norma brought Swedish meatballs and corn chowder. At Christmas in 1986, my ex-wife was in Florida with the kids, and I spent it with the Bondesons. We had a good meal, joked and talked. I think we had everything traditional except the lutefisk. Sandy Carlisle was there. I liked Sandy. He retired from the Navy reserve, sailed the U.S.S. *Constitution*. He was a salesman. He wasn't overly affectionate—not lovey-dovey kissy-huggy. I think illness drove a wedge between Sandy and Norma; she was always coming home to take care of her parents."

Jerry said he and Norma had spirited debates, many of them political. Norma's views were eclectic; as a nurse, she publicly endorsed a 1999 initiative to legalize medical marijuana in Maine.

"On social issues, Norma and I are in tune," Jerry said. "On spending and taxes, we probably are not that far apart. I try to get her wound up; I play devil's advocate. Politically she's to the right of me. She served during Desert Storm as a flight nurse and was in Saudi Arabia when the SCUD missiles hit. She impresses me as being the type of person who would take control and do what had to be done.

"I rode with Norma down to Bangor right before the poisoning. I had bus tickets to go to Virginia; Norma was going to Calumet. We talked about family. The church was having a rough time raising money for a minister, and we talked about what the church should do. She felt the church should share a minister. 'We have to remember it's not all Swedes anymore,' she said. 'You've got to get members outside of the Swedish community.' She wasn't any more upset at the church than anyone else was at times.

"Norma's beliefs and perseverance amaze me. Anything she decided to do, she could. She was commander of her unit. She's a lot like her mother in some ways. She can be stubborn."

Early one afternoon in February, Norma came into Stan's, sat down with some locals, and ordered a BLT sandwich and coffee. She talked about Harriet the pig and pondered whether to keep her in the chicken coop or the barn. She opened her napkin and filled it with the potato chips that came with her lunch. It was a snack for Harriet.

"Harriet is getting very big—very big," Sally Sandstrom later said, laughing. "I have a son, and my son plays with Finn. We take him up to the farm, and he plays with Harriet. Norma is like Finn's grandmother. I know she saves everything for Harriet. They were going to slaughter her, but they couldn't do it, so she's going to have piglets. Norma wouldn't hurt anybody."

There are more than a few people who agree with Sally. Ralph Ostlund, who was in a coma for two weeks after the poisoning, becomes very upset over the accusations against Norma. "Norma is a friend of mine," he said. "I don't think she'd hurt anyone." In fact, one Sunday after services at GA, Ralph approached Erica and quietly chastised her to be careful about what she said.

For a time, Norma thought about leaving Gustaf Adolph. "We've talked about this, Norma and I, and I've actually encouraged her not to give up," said Debbie Blanchette. "She said, 'I could go to Faith (Lutheran church in Caribou),' and I said, 'Why? This is your church, just like GA is my church, and don't you dare let them push you away. You have every right to be here.'"

"Norma is a woman of great backbone and, I think, a great deal of conscience," observed Pastor Jim Morgan, GA's interim pastor after Scottie Burkhalter left. "She and I, over time, had several opportunities to voice our independent ideas, which were not always in sync. And she was always very blunt and direct and had a strong wish for the well-being of the church, certainly, and I would say a very strong wish to maintain her own integrity. I always respected that."

A year after the poisoning, Pastor Morgan was asked by a reporter why he had such high regard for Norma. He paused for a moment and then spoke of an incident he had almost forgotten. It had happened only months before the poisoning.

"We were having a discussion about the safety of the furnace," he said. "And I talked about another church, where the furnace had been leaking carbon monoxide and had to be replaced. At her own expense, Norma quietly went out and bought carbon monoxide detectors and placed them around the church, just to make sure the furnace wasn't giving off any carbon monoxide. She was maintaining the safety of the church; she wanted to assure herself that everybody was safe."

Few, if any, GA members were aware that Norma had purchased the detectors, which a year later still hung on the walls inside the church. The police also knew nothing about it. "The police and I didn't have very many conversations about Norma," Pastor Morgan said. "I told them she wasn't on my list (of suspects)."

It seems illogical that the police would not have interviewed Pastor Morgan in great depth about his dealings with Norma, because the two had become very well acquainted. Was it because Morgan did not believe Norma was involved in the poisoning and thus did not support investigators' theories of her guilt? After all, detectives pressured church members to think long and hard about squabbles and feuds, no matter how small, and since Norma was involved in a good number of church issues and sometimes fiercely disagreed with her fellow members, her name kept coming up. As Sally Sandstrom pointed out, "She doesn't go along with the flow, and that makes her stand out."

The police pressed those who disliked Norma for more and more details about her behavior, which only served to bolster their suspicions about her possible involvement in the poisoning. Why did they not press Morgan just as hard about his confidence in her innocence? Had Morgan told the police about the carbon monoxide detectors early in the investigation, would Norma have been eliminated from suspicion? It would seem so. After all, what was the likelihood that a woman who had quietly taken special measures to protect the congregation from carbon monoxide poisoning would, only a few months later, poison that same congregation with arsenic?

"A lot of people are accusing Norma of having done it,"

said Lanie Wilson. "I know Norma very well, and I am pleased to say Norma is my friend. Norma didn't want to take over the church. Norma was not the problem there. The difference between Norma and these other people is they can't go to your face and tell you the problem. Let's say I have a bone to pick with you. If I disagree with you on something, I will go to your face and say, 'I don't agree with you.' Whereas with them, instead of doing that, they go behind your back and just stir it.

"Norma is a lot like her mother. She does not go behind your back if she dislikes you or disagrees with you. She will tell you right to your face. You don't hear it from a second person or a third person. Because Norma is vocal in how she feels, they figured that she wanted to run the show, but they're a hundred percent wrong. Norma's a sweet lady. I'm not her closest friend, but I'm a friend of the family, and you know, I've appreciated every one of them. Harold and Thorborg—I don't think God created any nicer people. I can't say enough good about the Bondesons because I really cherish them."

A Mission from God

For more than a year after the poisoning, Erica did not have a paying job; her vocation has been to care for her mother. She has also devoted hours to formulating a strategy to prevent a New Sweden massacre, envisioning scenarios where Norma Bondeson was often the villain, and Erica Grace was always the heroine.

"Say Norma or somebody comes in and pulls a gun, and I'm up in the balcony," Erica theorized. "I can call somebody from up there, get the police there, or I could get somebody to sneak in from the back, some of my friends. I have this all planned to a T. I've thought this all through. I have my cell phone right next to me, I've got friends that are actually uniformed cops, not detectives, but uniformed cops, and I have my cell phone handy. I've got numbers programmed in, my friends, and I've got numbers of people who live in the area who could rush, whatever they have to do.

"I just don't know what she's going to do, and that's the worst part. If I knew what she's capable of, I'd be more ready for it. But she will crack. I can see her coming back and there being a sequel. Not arsenic though, not arsenic. I can see her being more creative because she knows—she's not a stupid woman. She'll say she's dumb, but she's not a stupid woman. She knows that we look; she knows we're aware. People know what it tastes like. They know if the coffee tastes funny, don't drink it. She knows that, so if she's going to do something, she's going to do something different. But she may be very low key on it, or she may come out with a gun and start shooting. I don't know. I'm not sure of what this woman is thinking right now.

"I can picture her possibly doing something to come back at me. And even if I can get her on a little something, like trespassing or breaking into the house or something like that, something small, they've got enough to prosecute her, make her sweat, and then I'll go in and torment her every day until she just goes apeshit. So I have ways that I'm thinking this through, but I'm going to do everything I can to make her crazy. So I believe that, and I'm going to do everything I have to. I'll get in her face every Sunday if I have to.

"I've told Karla, and I've made the comment to Herman and Karla and my parents, if we go to church on Sunday, and Sally and Debbie and Norma are not there, I'm not staying, because everybody she likes is not there.

"I will find a way to make this woman crack, because she's not taking this shit to her grave. Our thing is, if she ever does crack and come out with the truth, well then, is it really the truth? You can always wonder . . . And I still say I'm on a mission from God."

It is also possible that Erica's mission is from an overactive imagination and from a police investigation that jumped the gun in concluding that the poisoning was a conspiracy.

There are several reasons why some investigators were convinced that Daniel Bondeson had not acted alone, the first being that his note began with the words "I acted alone. I acted alone." Why, detectives reasoned, would he feel the need to say that, let alone say it twice? Their conclusion: Because he had not acted alone. In other words, to paraphrase Shakespeare, the gentleman doth protest too much.

A more reasonable conclusion is easy to reach, given some of the facts. Carl Bondeson told police that on the morning of Danny's death, Carl, Norma, and Danny were all at the Bondeson farmhouse, and Norma was complaining that police thought she was involved in the poisoning.

The Bondesons are known, like most Swedes, to be a very close family, fiercely protective of one another, so it is quite possible that Danny had confessed to Carl and Norma that it was he who had poisoned the coffee. Just hours earlier, on Thursday night, Norma had undergone an interrogation by police about her involvement with the church, and now she was a suspect. Chances are she was angry with Danny about that, and who wouldn't be? He had committed an unthinkable crime for which Norma was now being blamed. If Norma and Carl were chastising him that morning, justifiably furious at what he had done, might not Danny have killed himself out of guilt and written the note, emphasizing that he acted alone, in order to clear his sister?

Another factor in the supposed case against Norma is a statement police said that she made during an interview: "I will take what I know to my grave." Police shared this comment with several of the arsenic survivors, and along with it went the connotation of Norma's guilt. But again, the Bondesons are a close and protective family. If Danny had confessed the details of his crime to Norma and Carl, why would they tell the police, who were likely to spill the beans to the media? The ugly saga of Danny's actions and his motive, which he probably also shared with Norma and Carl, would be splashed all over the newspaper and TV, embarrassing the Bondeson family as well as Danny's memory. Just as his attorney would not violate confidentiality, even posthumously, neither would his siblings.

The vilification of Norma Bondeson, the unproven belief that "she is a killer," as one cop put it, evolved over the course of an investigation with dubious methods of uncovering the truth. It was like a gust of wind, gradually gathering dust and then spinning into a tornado of accusation so powerful it could not be stopped.

What appears to have happened is this: From the beginning, police coaxed church members into dredging up every squabble and fight, every insult, every slight, "even if it seemed insignificant," as Appleton said, and then urged them to name possible suspects. Because of her forceful personality, and because certain people strongly disliked her, the name most often mentioned was Norma Bondeson. Danny's death, his cryptic suicide note, and certain investigators' allure for the mysterious gave the storm momentum, and byzantine scenarios and reckless accusations followed. After the first few weeks, the investigation stalled. Eighteen months after the crime, it remains so.

Closing the Door

In February 2004, after almost three years without pastoral leadership, Gustaf Adolph members welcomed the Reverend John Drever from Waterville, about four hours south. February 29 was the pastor's first service before his new congregation. Four church members—Ed and Leslie Margeson and Janet and Shirley Erickson—volunteered to make the coffee and bring refreshments.

Before the poisoning, the large pull-down door between the Sunday school and the church had been kept closed during the service. After the incident, to soothe jangled nerves, the door was kept open, the coffeepot clearly in sight.

When Debbie Blanchette arrived at the church for Pastor Drever's debut, she was surprised to see that the door was once again closed. *I'm so happy to see that door down*, she thought. *I'm so glad not to see the coffeepot.*

"Then Fran goes to Leslie and Ed and says, 'How come that door is down?'" Debbie recalled. "She said, 'Why isn't the door open so we can see the coffeepot?' And Dick went to Shirley and Janet: 'We're not having coffee; we're not going to drink that coffee. There's something wrong.'"

The issue was raised at the next church council meeting, Debbie said, when Ed Margeson brought it up. "He said, 'We'd like to know what your feelings are concerning keeping the doors closed. What do you want to do?'"

According to Debbie, about a half dozen council members said they would prefer to keep the door closed, including Bob Bengston, who, along with his parents, had drunk the poisoned coffee but had not become as seriously ill as some of the others. "Personally, I'm glad to see the door closed," he said. "It was horrible; it happened, but we need to move on. We can't keep looking back at this."

Shirley, who had drunk only a sip of the tainted coffee, agreed. "I want the door closed," she said.

Shirley's brother Oscar concurred, saying, "I'm glad that door is closed."

"Arline, Oscar, and I are probably the only ones on the council that didn't drink the coffee," Debbie recalled. "Arline said she was glad the door was closed because we need to look forward instead of continuing to look back. I said the same thing.

"We got down to the other end of the table. Karla said, 'I want that door open. I don't trust people in the congregation.' I'm thinking, *I know who the heck you're talking about, honey. Why don't you just say you don't trust Norma?* And Dale said, 'I want that door open. There's somebody in this congregation who was involved.'"

Finally, it was agreed that the door would remain open. Debbie was disappointed at first.

"Then when I got home and thought about it, I thought, I didn't drink the coffee; I'm not the one who's sick," she said. "And so hopefully there will come a time in the very near future when we can leave that door closed."

Debbie still finds it hard to believe that Danny poisoned the coffee, but she is beginning to accept that he probably did and to understand, perhaps, why he killed himself. "If he did this, yeah, he was sick," she said. "I couldn't see him going through a trial. There's no way. And yes, it's going to be horrible that you have to deal with his suicide, but for him to put his family through a trial and all that—no. So he took what he thought was the easy way out for his family."

The Christian Thing

The Sunday morning service that marked the first anniversary of the Gustaf Adolph arsenic poisoning was very low key. Pastor Drever did not mention the incident, but he did request two minutes of silence. Herman Fisher, standing piously erect in long, white, liturgical robes, served as lay minister. Only a handful of churchgoers attended, and only three reporters and two photographers were there. The photographers remained outside.

Fran and Dick Ruggles both appeared to be in good health. For a while Dick had been using a cane, but after many months, he no longer needed it. Fran, angry at the media's presence, turned around in her pew and shot a reporter a long, withering glare, and then stalked out of the church during communion, followed by her sister, Julie Adler. Five months later, said to be upset with the pastor for allowing reporters in the church, Fran had not returned, nor had Dick.

"Fran is very hurt," Beth Salisbury said. "I saw her after Melvin Adler died. She doesn't even look the same; she looks very hard. And she wasn't like that; I mean Fran would help anybody. She's just a very caring woman; she really is—both her and her husband. Fran made my wedding gown. She sat there and helped me make all the decorations; she decorated the church. She's a lot of fun; she's hilarious.

"I don't call her. I don't know what to say. I feel bad because I never called when everything happened. It sounds stupid, but it's a constant reminder that someone's still out there."

Lois attended the anniversary service with her husband, Carl, and several other family members; she, too, was looking well. She said her recovery had been slow and difficult, and she still had some bad days, but had enjoyed many wonderful times as well. "I have one daughter who takes me to something special every month," she said. "We went to Nova Scotia; we went to see Anne Murray and got backstage passes; we got to talk to her. It was so special. I actually laughed all by myself last month. It's taken me all this time to be happy again, as I was before."

What hurts so much, Lois said, was the fear that the people responsible for the poisoning would not be caught. "And they'll get to live their lives," she said, "and the rest of us don't know what our lives are going to be like. Are we going to have cancer? If they get away with this, I don't know—somehow it has to end. If they were to end it tomorrow, I could forgive whoever it was and get on with it. Until then I can't; I just want the truth to be told."

Dale Anderson, who nearly died in the emergency room, also attended the anniversary service, but had not done as well as some of the others. "My legs are bad; they hurt," he said. "My feet hurt, and I stumble a lot." He also has intestinal problems since the poisoning. "I'm not feeling good at all, and I just can't shake it," he said.

Ralph Ostlund, who also came close to death, seemed almost as good as new. He skied 150 miles over the winter and competed in a thirteen-mile race. Ralph had high blood pressure before the poisoning, but afterward, it was low enough to stop his medication. He took a trip to Florida in the spring, and attended the graduations of several of his grandchildren. He still suffers some pain in his legs, but danced every number at the pig roast.

Lester Beaupre decided to get out of town for the anniversary and went to Bangor with Louise. "I bought a twenty-one-speed bike to celebrate the day I almost got killed," he said. "It's from Toys R Us—a men's Mongoose bike. It's metallic grey and has all kinds of extras."

Lester was looking forward to the next men's group meeting; it was his week to bring the refreshments. "So I'm going to make my brown sugar pie," he said. "That's something my mother always used to make when I was a kid. She always made a small one, about six inches around. When she made her piecrust, whatever she had leftover, she'd make a brown sugar pie."

"I could never get the exact recipe; with my mother, it was a pinch of this and a pinch of that. So I went on this quest, and I made a whole bunch of pies until I made one that I liked. Now my recipe is in the Swedish cookbook on page 144: Three teaspoons of melted butter; two-thirds cup of brown sugar; one-third cup of flour; a teaspoon of vanilla, and one third cup of canned milk. Mix the butter, sugar, flour, and vanilla together, and then add the canned milk. Pour into an unbaked piecrust, put the top on the crust, and bake at 375 for ten minutes, then at 325 for twenty minutes or until brown.

"The ingredients are the same as my mother's, but I had to figure out the measurements. I've made some pretty bad pies—there were some that you had to shoot to eat. The main ingredients are brown sugar and flour—that's a pretty iffy deal there; it's going to go one way or the other. It's going to be hard to have something that has a good texture to it. I'm going to make one this weekend.

"I really like key lime pie. Two years ago Louise went to Florida with her mother and she got the real deal from Key West. She got the bottles of lime juice to make the pie. That was so good—so good. After that she bought other different brands, but it wasn't the same.

"You know who has good desserts? In Houlton when you get off I-95, that diner."

Lester said he would like to know what happened at the church, but was trying to let it go. "The detectives cried wolf, and now they can't find the wolf," he said. "They don't know what to do; they don't want to back out of it. They don't want to tell the world they assumed and were wrong. They're trying to bow out of this, but there are still a lot of people who want to know why the detectives said what they said. A lot of the population is still on edge because this case is not being solved or done away with. I just feel the police have to do as much with our anxiety as the crime itself."

Lester went back to work full time, but sometimes he knocks off early because of pain in his feet and legs. Late in the summer of 2004 he visited with Ellie Morrill. She had decided to sell her house.

"She took me down to Reid's workshop," Lester recalled, "and everything was the same as the day Reid passed away." Coats and work shirts still hung from wooden hooks on the wall. Reid's old hand drill lay on the table next to an unfinished project. "I felt like I was intruding," Lester said. "A man's workshop is such a personal thing." Ellie, he said, was planning to have a yard sale, but she just could not bring herself to do it.

Erich Margeson came to the anniversary service at church filled with gratitude; his wife, Alana, had just brought home their three new baby boys. The triplets had been born in March, and all were doing well. The smallest one had spent several weeks in an incubator, and the couple named him "Reid."

Herman was feeling good, but it had been a difficult journey. For several months after the poisoning, he would tire easily; after only two or three hours, he would have to lie down. That lasted most of the summer of 2003. "When Dan and Monica were here in July," Karla said, referring to Herman's son and daughter-in-law, "I had to really take charge, because Monica's real pushy."

By autumn of 2003, Herman was back on his job as a purchasing agent, was remodeling the family room in his house, and crooning the lead in a barbershop quartet. He said money was not an issue for any of the victims: "There's none of us that are hurting for medical bills."

In some respects, at least, Herman's life had improved. "The relationship with my daughter has become a lot better," he said. "We were having a hard time before this happened."

"They got along; they spoke, but they weren't close," Karla added, "but after that happened, she wouldn't leave his bedside. She was right there. And you know what? As far as I'm concerned, we've got the most important thing in the world. We've got him here."

On the evening of the anniversary, Herman and Karla hosted a party at their home. At least a dozen cars were parked bumper to bumper in their driveway and on the street in front of the house.

Just down the road, a lone white car was parked outside the church. It belonged to Norma.

Karla said she holds no hard feelings toward Danny. "If he helped by putting (the poison) in," she said, "it was only because Norma nagged him to the point where he couldn't live life comfortably at home."

Karla's remark typified the sentiments of many in New Sweden, who almost a year after the crime, still refused to blame Danny, instead pointing the accusatory finger at his sister. It was striking, in fact, how virtually no indignation was directed toward Danny, who had admitted in his suicide note that he alone was responsible for the crime, while so much wrath was targeted at Norma, against whom there has never been a trace of tangible evidence.

"I don't think certain people will ever let her come back to where she was," Sally Sandstrom said.

Despite this, Norma has gone on with life as usual. She attends church every Sunday, often with Finn. In September 2004, Harriet gave birth to seven piglets. "Norma was in Stan's the other day and had to go home to feed her," Jerry

Nelson said. "They'll never get rid of Harriet. They'll probably have to sell the piglets."

Jerry paused for a moment, and then continued. "I still find it awfully hard to believe that Danny did that," he said. "It's so sad to see what's happened. What's happened to Norma is an absolute disgrace. It's been rough on Carl, too. At the Midsommar Fisherman's Breakfast, I had Sven come down and help. That was acceptable, but then Carl came up to cook, and some people were cool to him. It was as though it was not acceptable to have Carl come."

Despite the lingering suspicions, the seemingly endless investigation, and the absence of closure, Herman Fisher claims to have resolved any feelings of anger. "Oh yeah, there was a point where I was plenty mad," he said, "but not anymore."

How would he feel if the case were solved? Herman was asked.

"If we knew who it was, we would probably forgive them," he replied. "We would do the Christian thing—just like we've been doing all along."

Afterword

The New Sweden arsenic poisoning had far-reaching effects on public health policies and medical research, including a major change in the allocation of federal bioterrorism funds.

Before the poisoning, states were not allowed to use those funds to purchase stockpiles of antibiotics and chemical antidotes; the federal government had planned instead to establish regional supplies that would be delivered where needed within twelve hours. But as the New Sweden incident illustrated, chemical poisonings demand immediate treatment. Fortunately, Maine Bureau of Health Director Dr. Dora Mills had circumvented the federal government and used the state's homeland security funds to purchase the antidotes, so when the incident happened, the drugs were already in Maine. Early treatment with those antidotes saved victims' lives and helped to minimize damage to their internal organs.

Administrators from the federal Department of Homeland Security reviewed Maine's response several weeks after the poisoning and acknowledged the benefit of having local supplies of antidotes. This led to the revision of federal bioterrorism guidelines, and the government urged each state to create their own pharmaceutical stockpiles.

In another stroke of good timing, Maine had recently purchased new conference-call technology with bioterrorism funds, speeding up communications and response to the poisoning.

Responders to the New Sweden arsenic poisonings began collaboration on a case study for publication in a major medical journal, and medical researchers previously hindered by a lack of data on arsenic now say the incident will help them rewrite textbooks on toxicology. Because of it, doctors have a better chance of quickly identifying arsenic poisoning and have more information about symptoms and what they mean. Dale and Lois Anderson's experience taught doctors that arsenic is absorbed by dentures, which become permanently contaminated and must be replaced. Information from the church poisoning will also be included in a chapter on arsenic in a reference book commonly used in hospital emergency rooms.